RETROVIRUS

WRITTEN & CREATED BY

JUSTIN GRAY &
JIMMY PALMIOTTI

ARTWORK BY

NORBERTO FERNANDEZ

COVER BY

AMANDA CONNER

LETTERED & DESIGNED BY

BILL TORTOLINI

EDITED BY

JOANNE STARER

IMAGE COMICS, INC.
Robert Kirkman - chief operating officer
Erik Larsen - chief financial officer
Todd McFarlane - president
Marc Silvestri - chief executive officer
Jim Valentino - vice-president
Eric Stephenson - publisher
Todd Martinez - sales & licensing coordinator
Jennifer de Guzman - pr & marketing director
Branwyn Bigglestone - accounts manager
Emily Miller - administrative assistant
Jamie Parreno - marketing assistant
Sarah deLaine - events coordinator
Kevin Yuen - digital rights coordinator
Jonathan Chan - production manager
Drew Gill - art director
Monica Garcia - production artist
Vincent Kukua - production artist
Jana Cook - production artist
www.imagecomics.com

PAPER FILMS

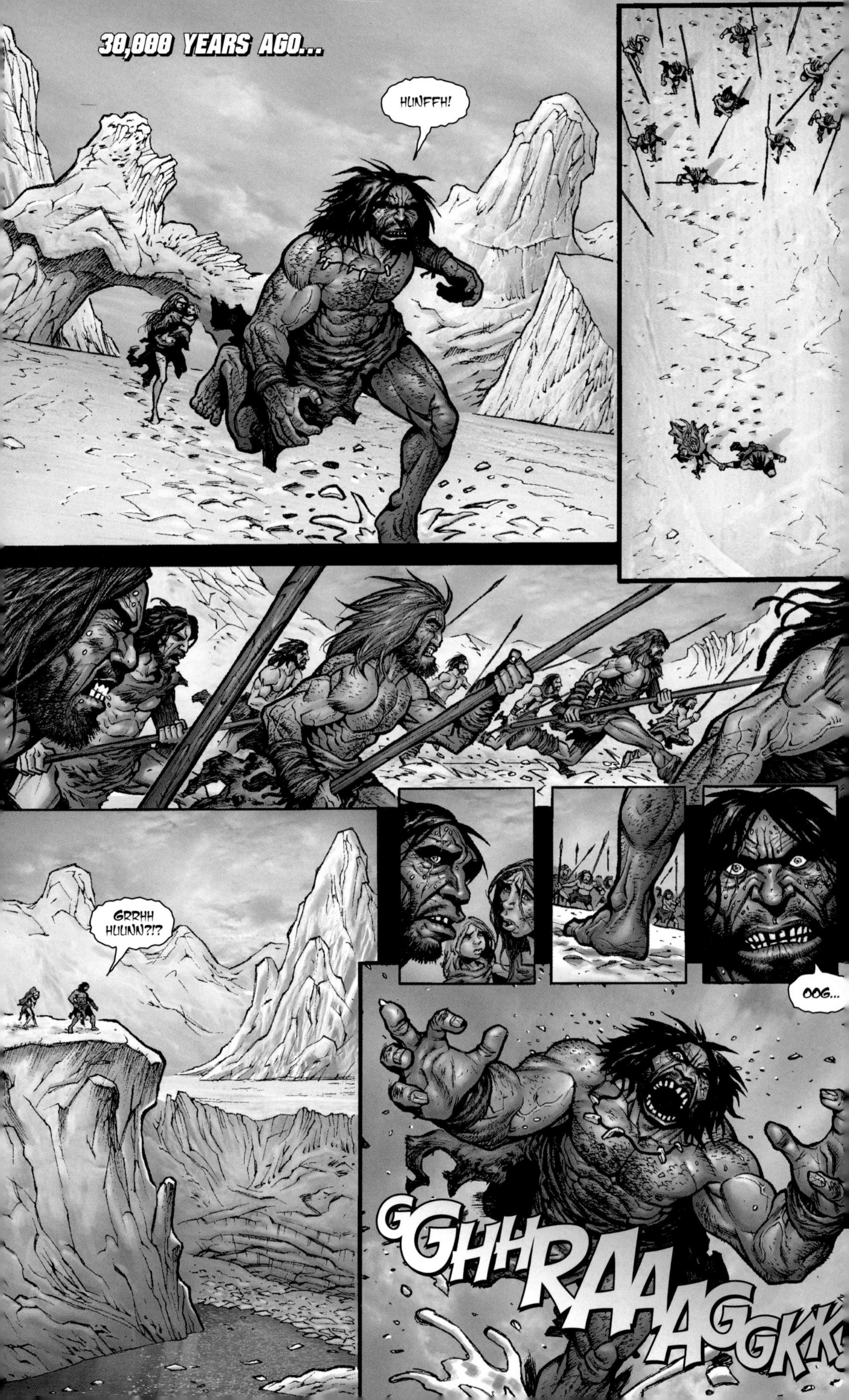
30,000 YEARS AGO...
HUNFFH!
GRRHH HUUNN?!?
OOG...
GGHHRAAAGKK!

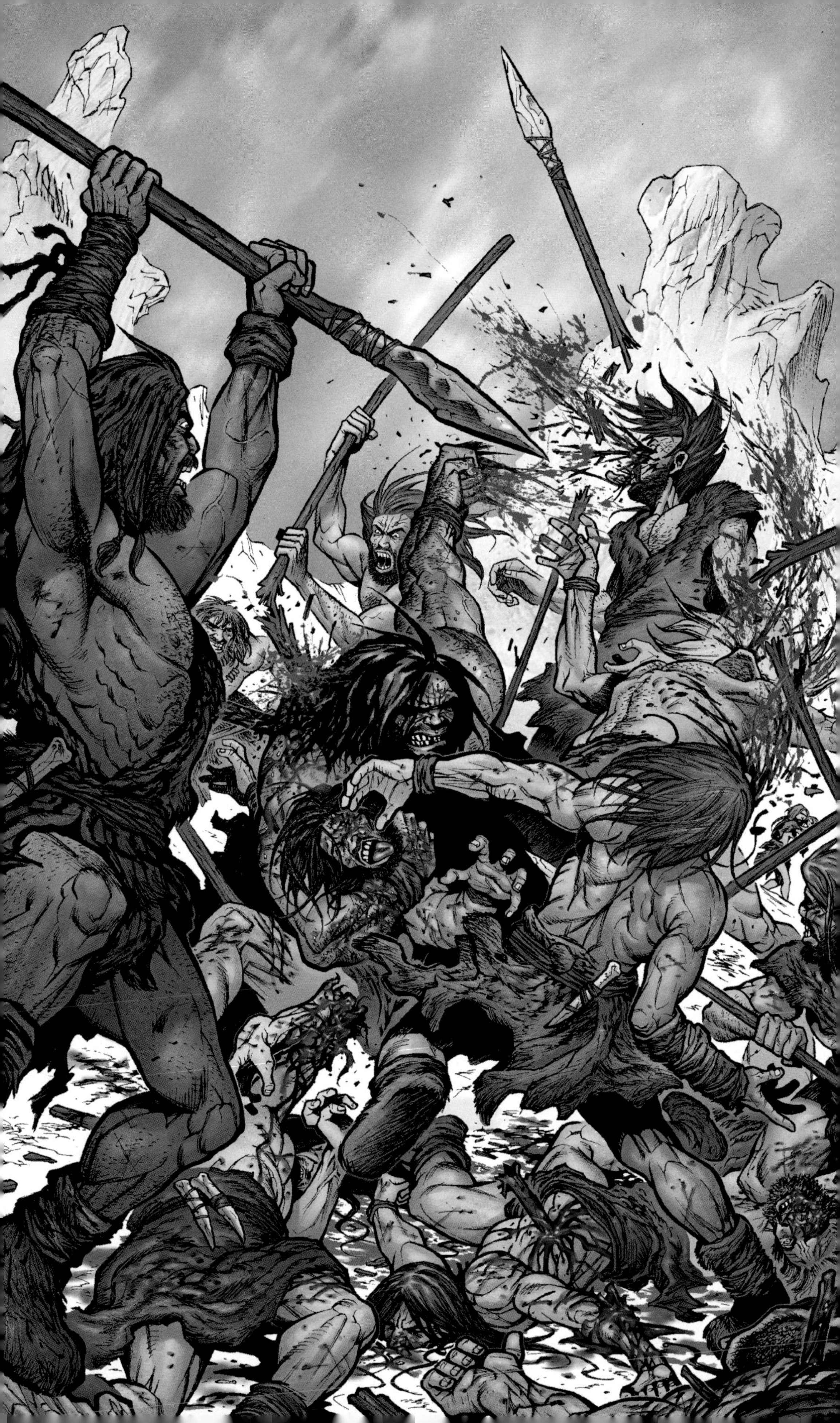

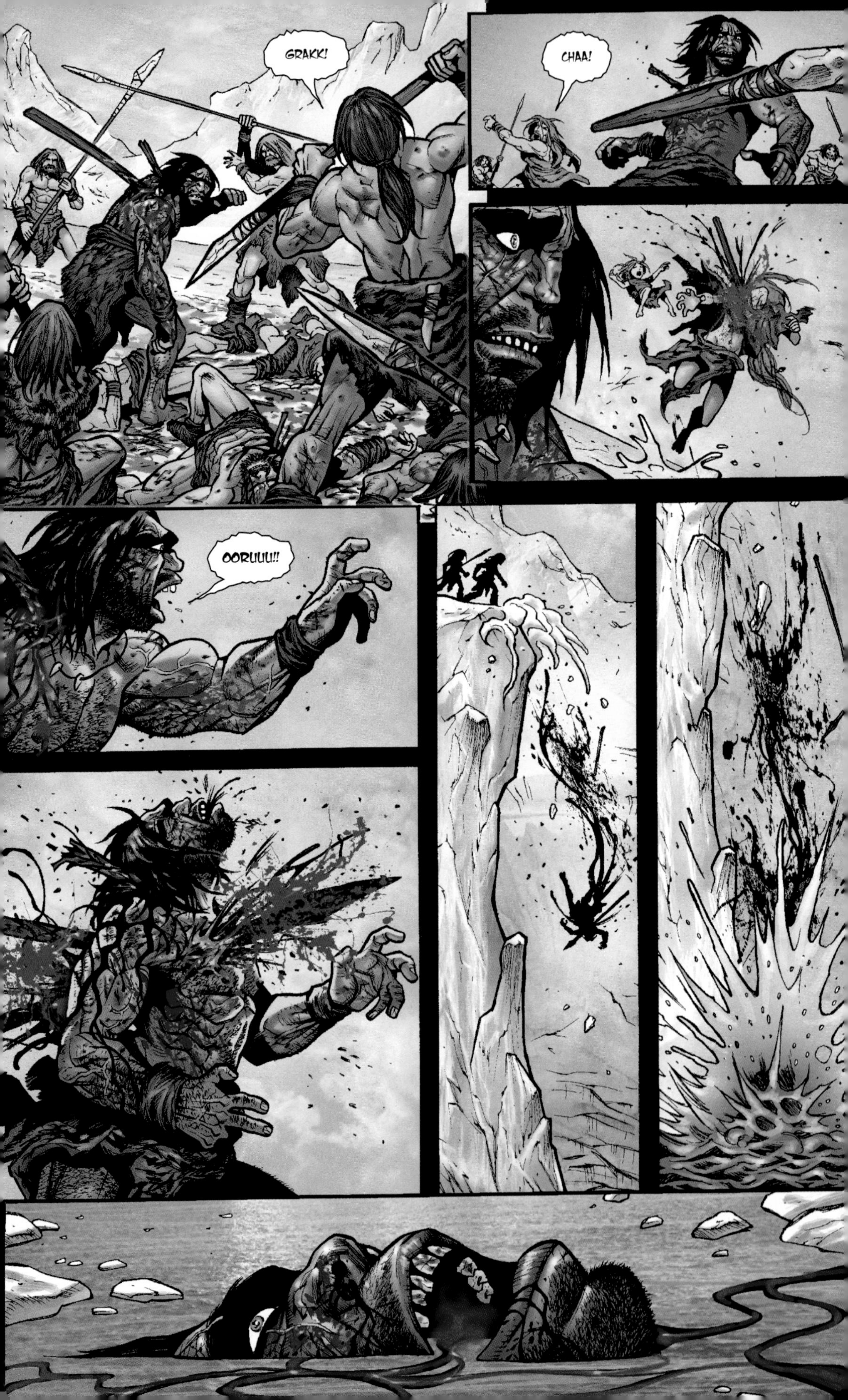
GRAKK!
CHAA!
OORUUU!!

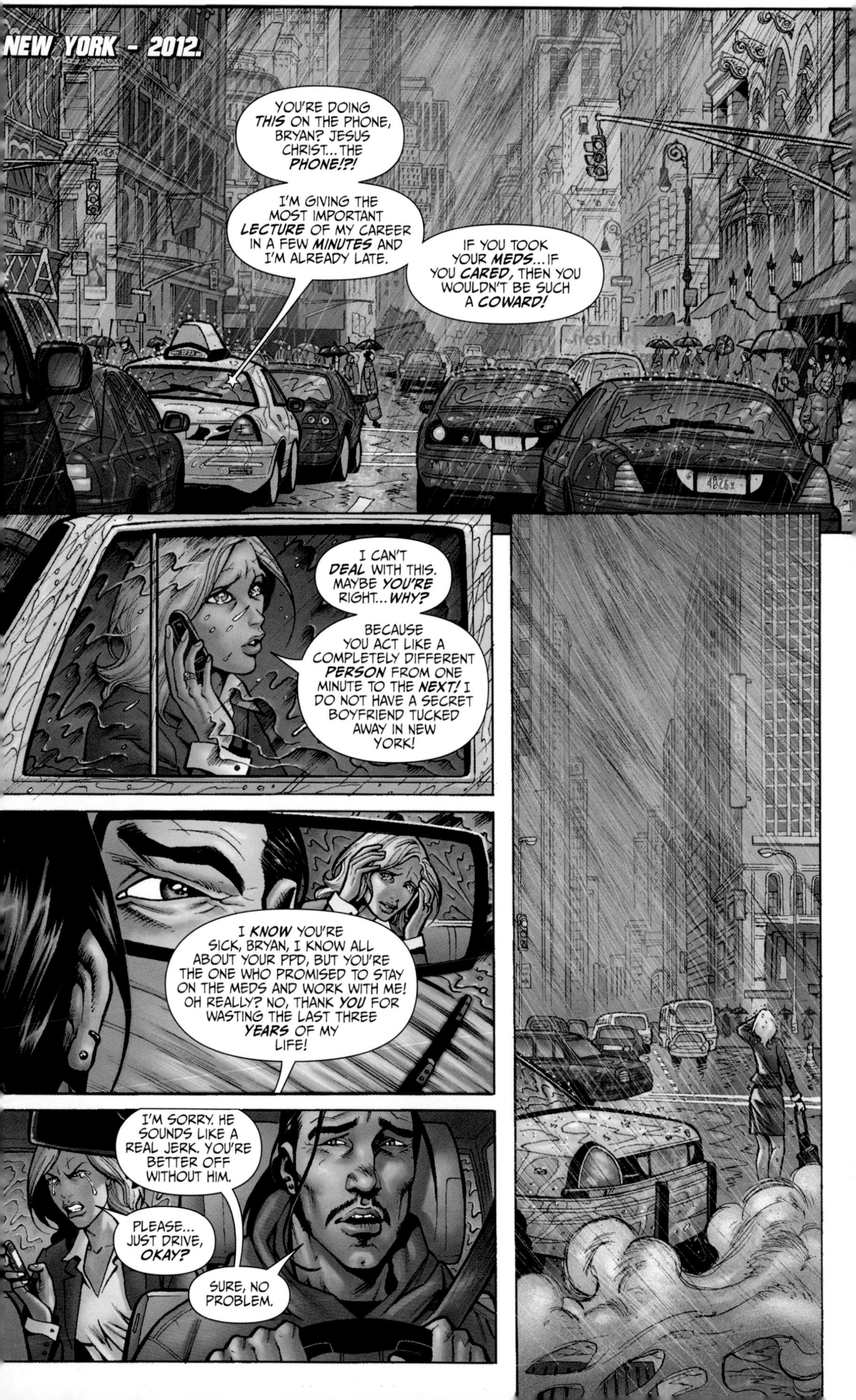
NEW YORK - 2012.
YOU'RE DOING THIS ON THE PHONE, BRYAN? JESUS CHRIST... THE PHONE!?!
I'M GIVING THE MOST IMPORTANT LECTURE OF MY CAREER IN A FEW MINUTES AND I'M ALREADY LATE.
IF YOU TOOK YOUR MEDS... IF YOU CARED, THEN YOU WOULDN'T BE SUCH A COWARD!
I CAN'T DEAL WITH THIS. MAYBE YOU'RE RIGHT... WHY?
BECAUSE YOU ACT LIKE A COMPLETELY DIFFERENT PERSON FROM ONE MINUTE TO THE NEXT! I DO NOT HAVE A SECRET BOYFRIEND TUCKED AWAY IN NEW YORK!
I KNOW YOU'RE SICK, BRYAN, I KNOW ALL ABOUT YOUR PPD, BUT YOU'RE THE ONE WHO PROMISED TO STAY ON THE MEDS AND WORK WITH ME! OH REALLY? NO, THANK YOU FOR WASTING THE LAST THREE YEARS OF MY LIFE!
I'M SORRY. HE SOUNDS LIKE A REAL JERK. YOU'RE BETTER OFF WITHOUT HIM.
PLEASE... JUST DRIVE, OKAY?
SURE, NO PROBLEM.

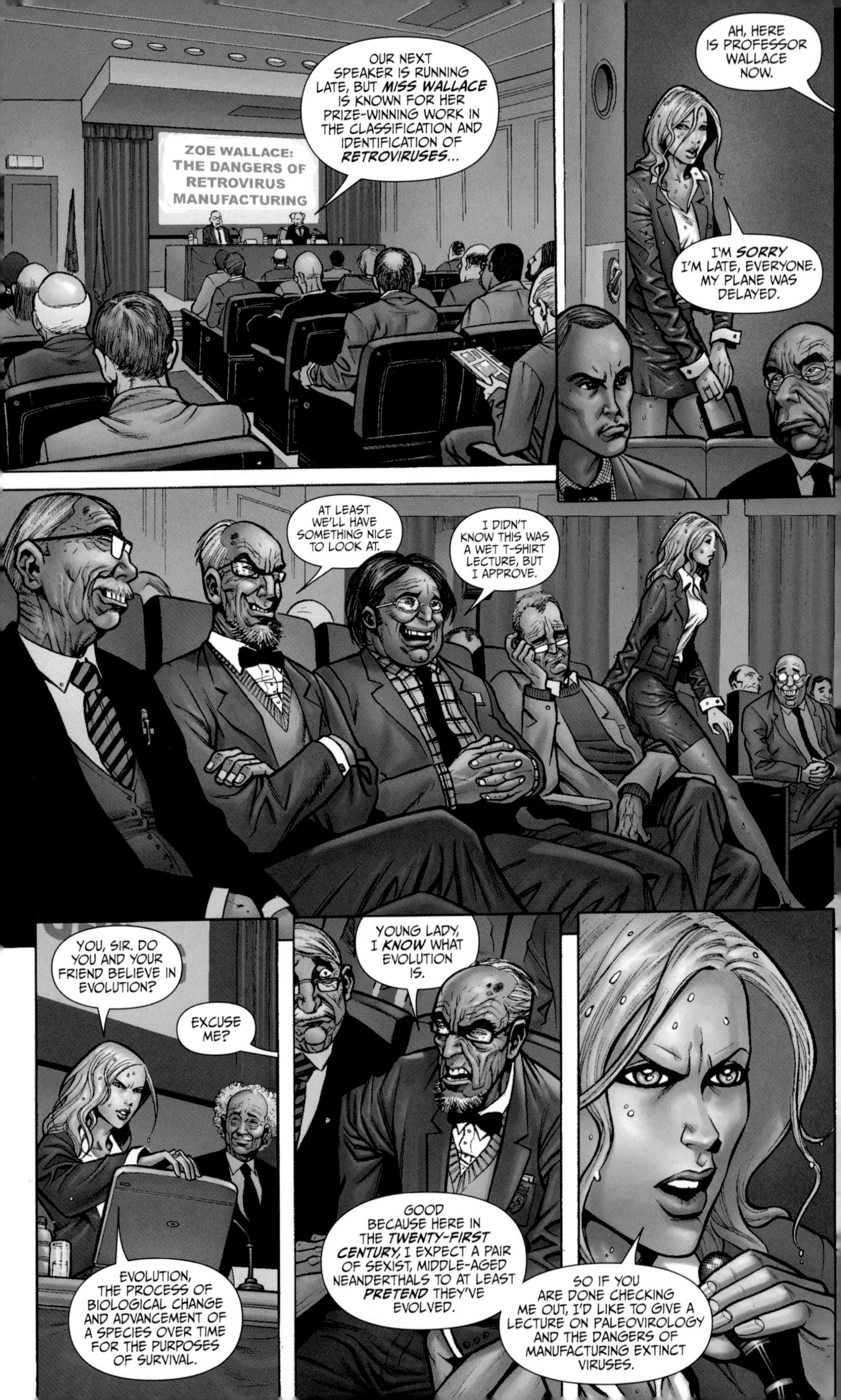
ZOE WALLACE: THE DANGERS OF RETROVIRUS MANUFACTURING
OUR NEXT SPEAKER IS RUNNING LATE, BUT MISS WALLACE IS KNOWN FOR HER PRIZE-WINNING WORK IN THE CLASSIFICATION AND IDENTIFICATION OF RETROVIRUSES...
AH, HERE IS PROFESSOR WALLACE NOW.
I'M SORRY I'M LATE, EVERYONE. MY PLANE WAS DELAYED.
AT LEAST WE'LL HAVE SOMETHING NICE TO LOOK AT.
I DIDN'T KNOW THIS WAS A WET T-SHIRT LECTURE, BUT I APPROVE.
YOU, SIR. DO YOU AND YOUR FRIEND BELIEVE IN EVOLUTION?
EXCUSE ME?
EVOLUTION, THE PROCESS OF BIOLOGICAL CHANGE AND ADVANCEMENT OF A SPECIES OVER TIME FOR THE PURPOSES OF SURVIVAL.
YOUNG LADY, I KNOW WHAT EVOLUTION IS.
GOOD BECAUSE HERE IN THE TWENTY-FIRST CENTURY, I EXPECT A PAIR OF SEXIST, MIDDLE-AGED NEANDERTHALS TO AT LEAST PRETEND THEY'VE EVOLVED.
SO IF YOU ARE DONE CHECKING ME OUT, I'D LIKE TO GIVE A LECTURE ON PALEOVIROLOGY AND THE DANGERS OF MANUFACTURING EXTINCT VIRUSES.

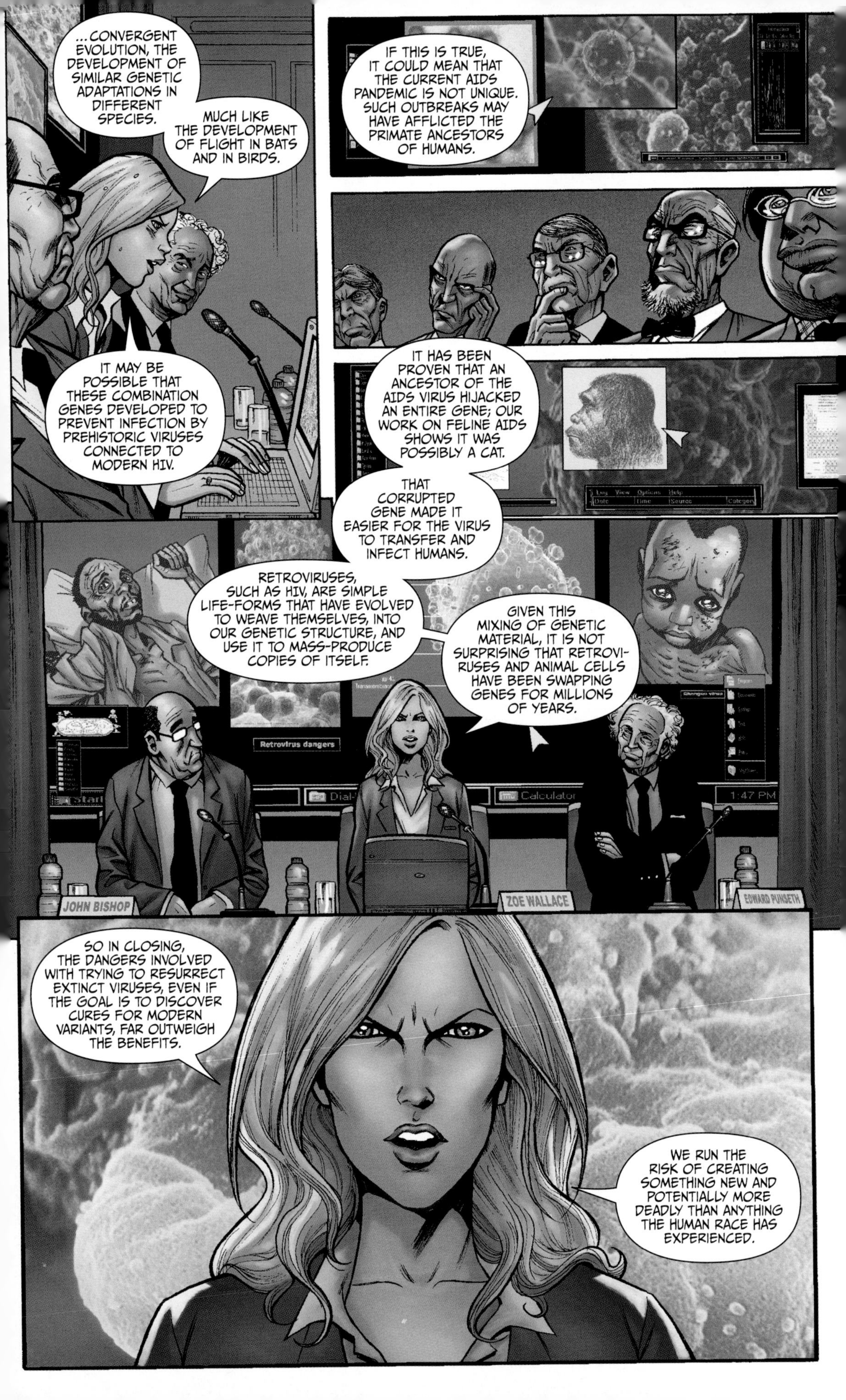
...CONVERGENT EVOLUTION, THE DEVELOPMENT OF SIMILAR GENETIC ADAPTATIONS IN DIFFERENT SPECIES.
MUCH LIKE THE DEVELOPMENT OF FLIGHT IN BATS AND IN BIRDS.
IT MAY BE POSSIBLE THAT THESE COMBINATION GENES DEVELOPED TO PREVENT INFECTION BY PREHISTORIC VIRUSES CONNECTED TO MODERN HIV.
IF THIS IS TRUE, IT COULD MEAN THAT THE CURRENT AIDS PANDEMIC IS NOT UNIQUE. SUCH OUTBREAKS MAY HAVE AFFLICTED THE PRIMATE ANCESTORS OF HUMANS.
IT HAS BEEN PROVEN THAT AN ANCESTOR OF THE AIDS VIRUS HIJACKED AN ENTIRE GENE; OUR WORK ON FELINE AIDS SHOWS IT WAS POSSIBLY A CAT.
THAT CORRUPTED GENE MADE IT EASIER FOR THE VIRUS TO TRANSFER AND INFECT HUMANS.
RETROVIRUSES, SUCH AS HIV, ARE SIMPLE LIFE-FORMS THAT HAVE EVOLVED TO WEAVE THEMSELVES, INTO OUR GENETIC STRUCTURE, AND USE IT TO MASS-PRODUCE COPIES OF ITSELF.
GIVEN THIS MIXING OF GENETIC MATERIAL, IT IS NOT SURPRISING THAT RETROVIRUSES AND ANIMAL CELLS HAVE BEEN SWAPPING GENES FOR MILLIONS OF YEARS.
Retrovirus dangers
Calculator
1:47 PM
JOHN BISHOP
ZOE WALLACE
EDWARD PUNSETH
SO IN CLOSING, THE DANGERS INVOLVED WITH TRYING TO RESURRECT EXTINCT VIRUSES, EVEN IF THE GOAL IS TO DISCOVER CURES FOR MODERN VARIANTS, FAR OUTWEIGH THE BENEFITS.
WE RUN THE RISK OF CREATING SOMETHING NEW AND POTENTIALLY MORE DEADLY THAN ANYTHING THE HUMAN RACE HAS EXPERIENCED.

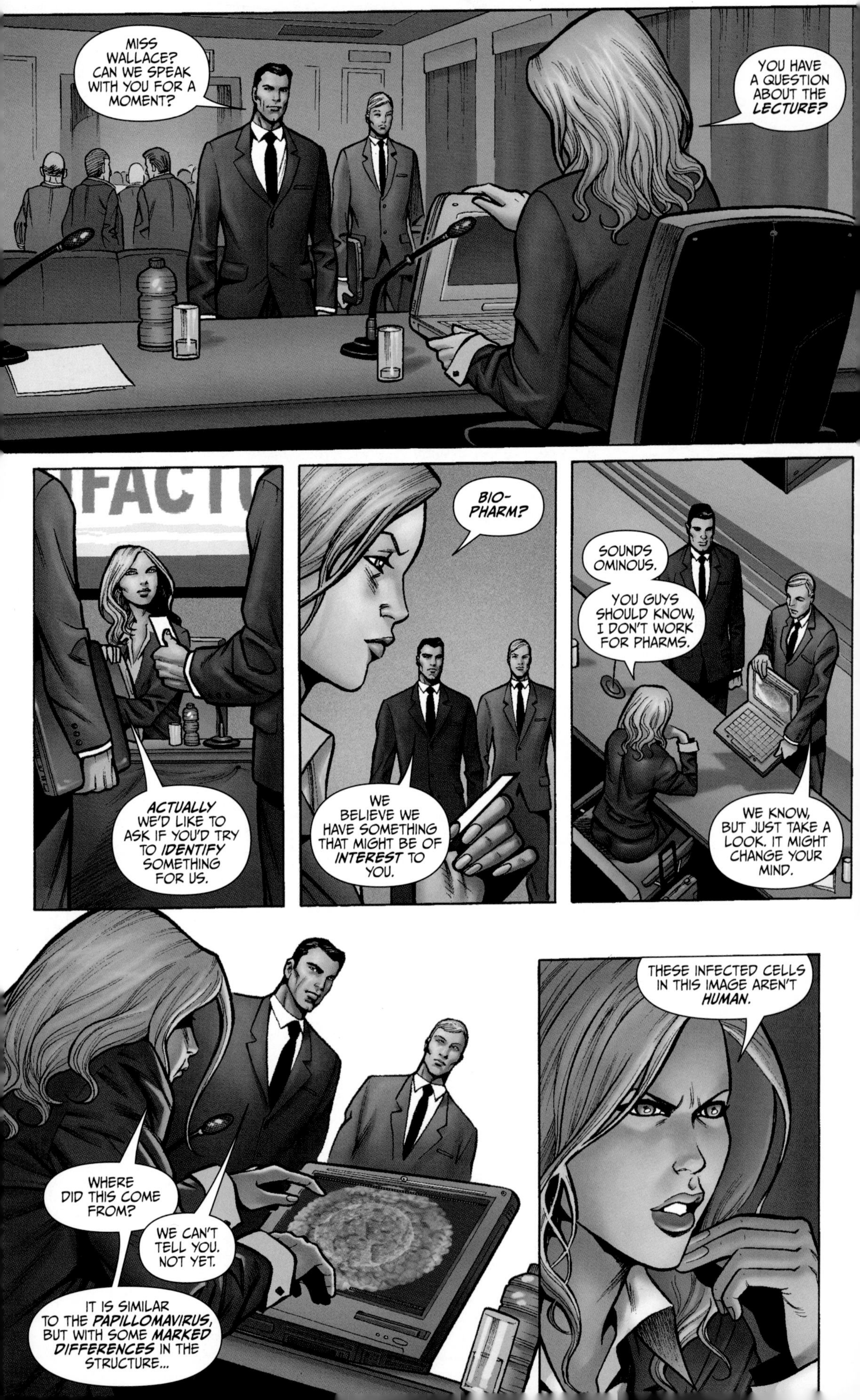

MISS WALLACE? CAN WE SPEAK WITH YOU FOR A MOMENT?
YOU HAVE A QUESTION ABOUT THE *LECTURE?*
IFACT
ACTUALLY WE'D LIKE TO ASK IF YOU'D TRY TO *IDENTIFY* SOMETHING FOR US.
BIO-PHARM?
WE BELIEVE WE HAVE SOMETHING THAT MIGHT BE OF *INTEREST* TO YOU.
SOUNDS OMINOUS.
YOU GUYS SHOULD KNOW, I DON'T WORK FOR PHARMS.
WE KNOW, BUT JUST TAKE A LOOK. IT MIGHT CHANGE YOUR MIND.
WHERE DID THIS COME FROM?
WE CAN'T TELL YOU. NOT YET.
IT IS SIMILAR TO THE *PAPILLOMAVIRUS,* BUT WITH SOME *MARKED DIFFERENCES* IN THE STRUCTURE...
THESE INFECTED CELLS IN THIS IMAGE AREN'T *HUMAN.*

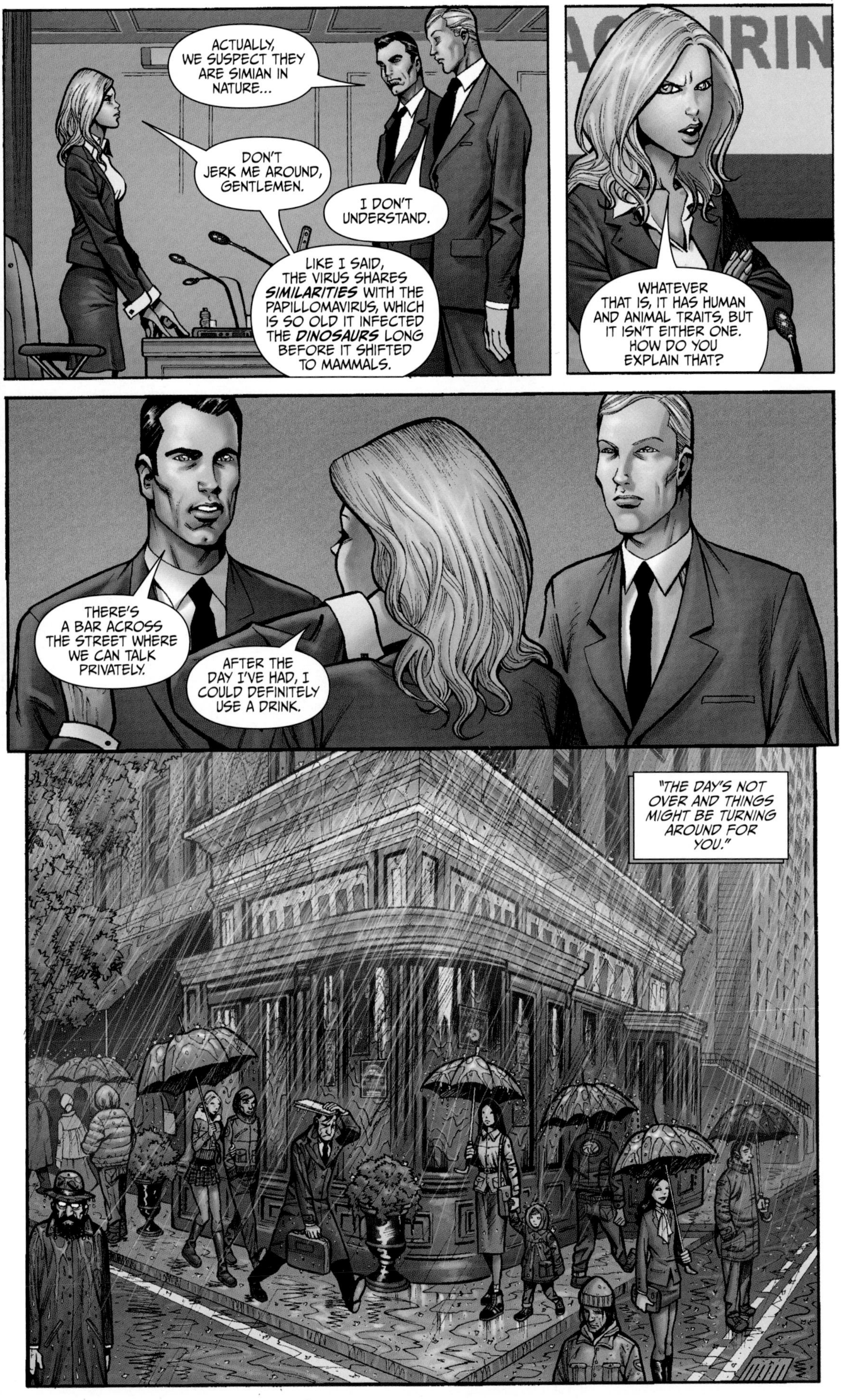
ACTUALLY, WE SUSPECT THEY ARE SIMIAN IN NATURE...
DON'T JERK ME AROUND, GENTLEMEN.
I DON'T UNDERSTAND.
LIKE I SAID, THE VIRUS SHARES SIMILARITIES WITH THE PAPILLOMAVIRUS, WHICH IS SO OLD IT INFECTED THE DINOSAURS LONG BEFORE IT SHIFTED TO MAMMALS.
WHATEVER THAT IS, IT HAS HUMAN AND ANIMAL TRAITS, BUT IT ISN'T EITHER ONE. HOW DO YOU EXPLAIN THAT?
THERE'S A BAR ACROSS THE STREET WHERE WE CAN TALK PRIVATELY.
AFTER THE DAY I'VE HAD, I COULD DEFINITELY USE A DRINK.
"THE DAY'S NOT OVER AND THINGS MIGHT BE TURNING AROUND FOR YOU."

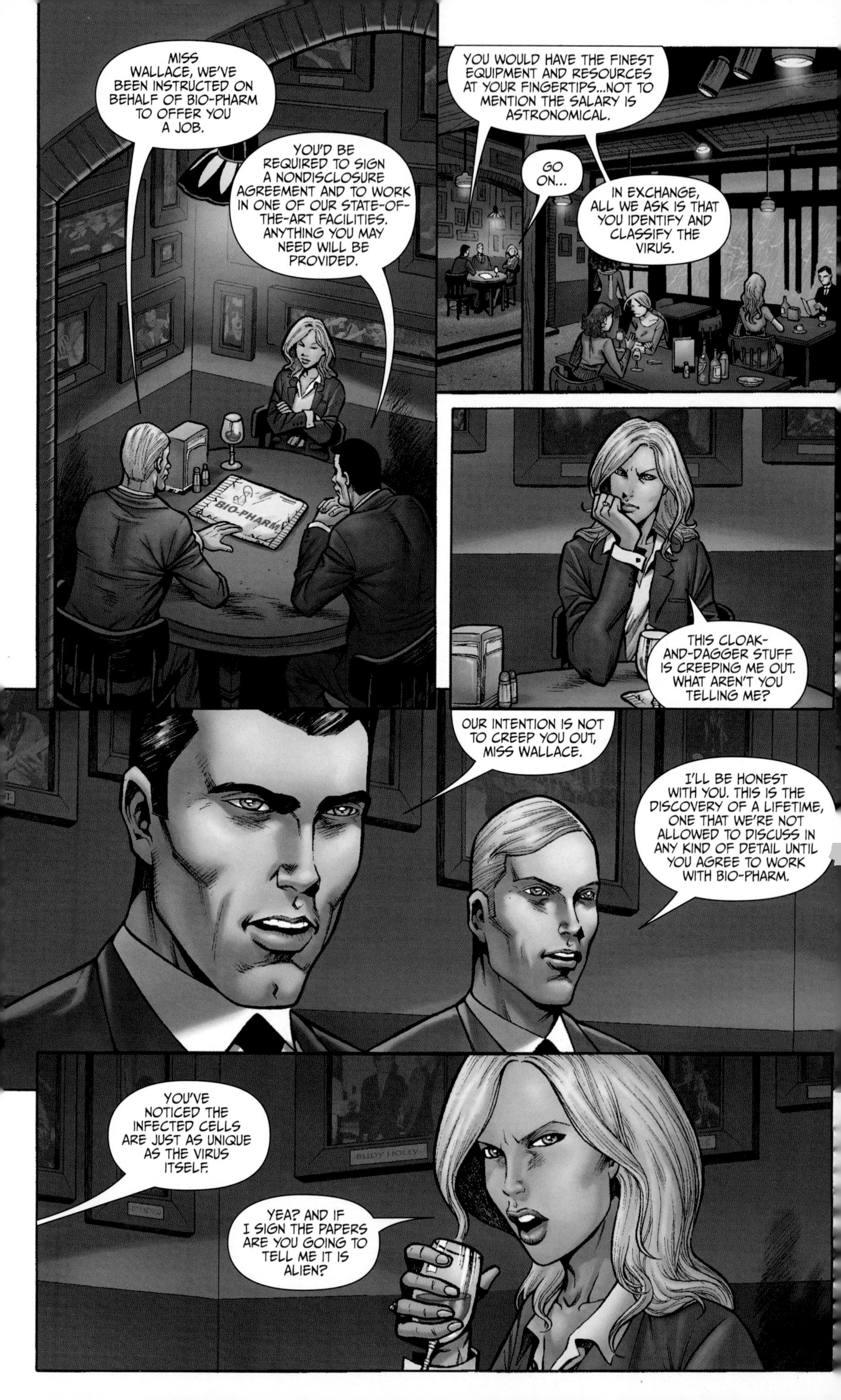
MISS WALLACE, WE'VE BEEN INSTRUCTED ON BEHALF OF BIO-PHARM TO OFFER YOU A JOB.
YOU'D BE REQUIRED TO SIGN A NONDISCLOSURE AGREEMENT AND TO WORK IN ONE OF OUR STATE-OF-THE-ART FACILITIES. ANYTHING YOU MAY NEED WILL BE PROVIDED.
BIO-PHARM
YOU WOULD HAVE THE FINEST EQUIPMENT AND RESOURCES AT YOUR FINGERTIPS...NOT TO MENTION THE SALARY IS ASTRONOMICAL.
GO ON...
IN EXCHANGE, ALL WE ASK IS THAT YOU IDENTIFY AND CLASSIFY THE VIRUS.
THIS CLOAK-AND-DAGGER STUFF IS CREEPING ME OUT. WHAT AREN'T YOU TELLING ME?
OUR INTENTION IS NOT TO CREEP YOU OUT, MISS WALLACE.
I'LL BE HONEST WITH YOU. THIS IS THE DISCOVERY OF A LIFETIME, ONE THAT WE'RE NOT ALLOWED TO DISCUSS IN ANY KIND OF DETAIL UNTIL YOU AGREE TO WORK WITH BIO-PHARM.
YOU'VE NOTICED THE INFECTED CELLS ARE JUST AS UNIQUE AS THE VIRUS ITSELF.
BUDDY HOLLY
YEA? AND IF I SIGN THE PAPERS ARE YOU GOING TO TELL ME IT IS ALIEN?

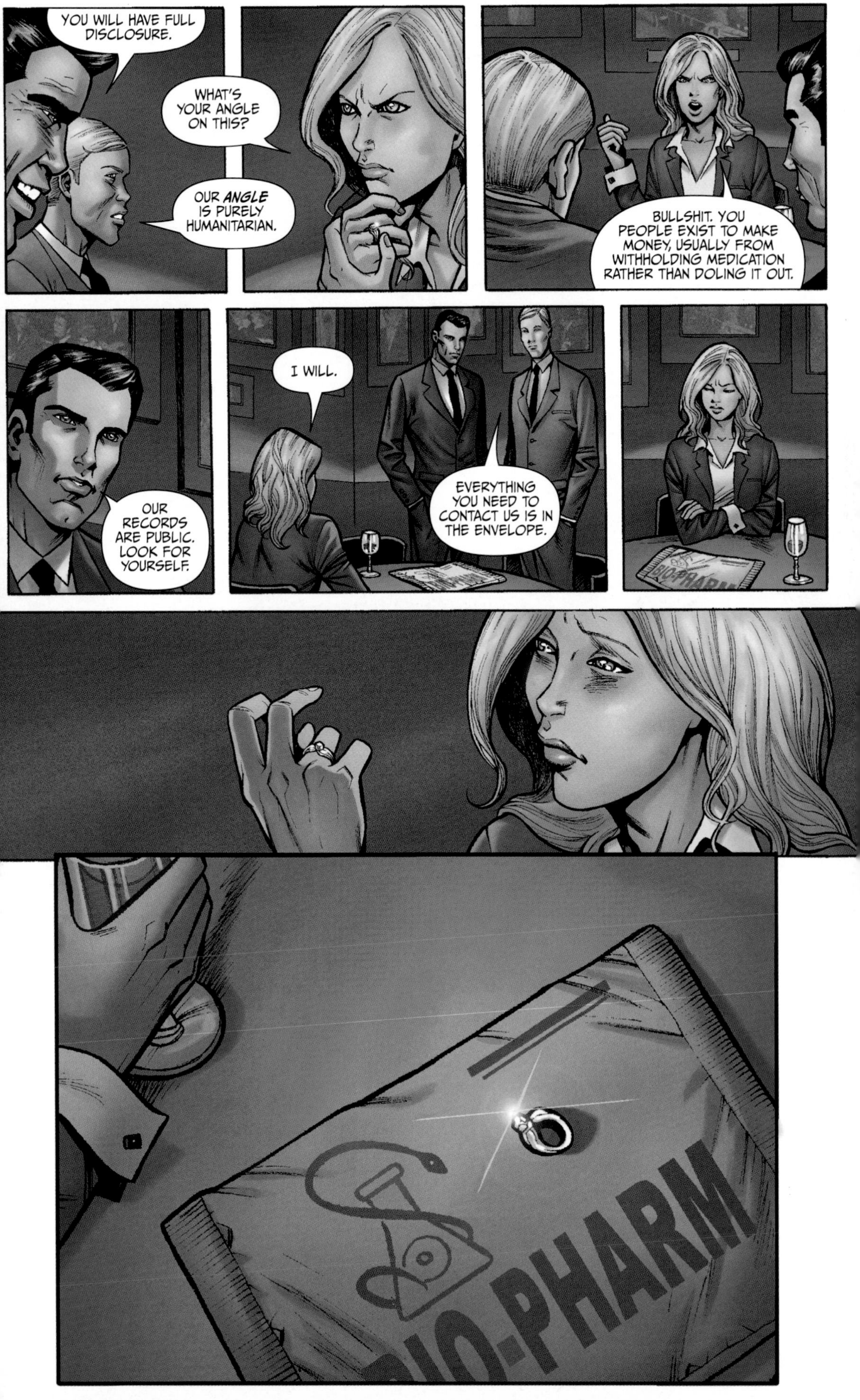
YOU WILL HAVE FULL DISCLOSURE.
WHAT'S YOUR ANGLE ON THIS?
OUR ANGLE IS PURELY HUMANITARIAN.
BULLSHIT. YOU PEOPLE EXIST TO MAKE MONEY, USUALLY FROM WITHHOLDING MEDICATION RATHER THAN DOLING IT OUT.
OUR RECORDS ARE PUBLIC. LOOK FOR YOURSELF.
I WILL.
EVERYTHING YOU NEED TO CONTACT US IS IN THE ENVELOPE.
BIO-PHARM

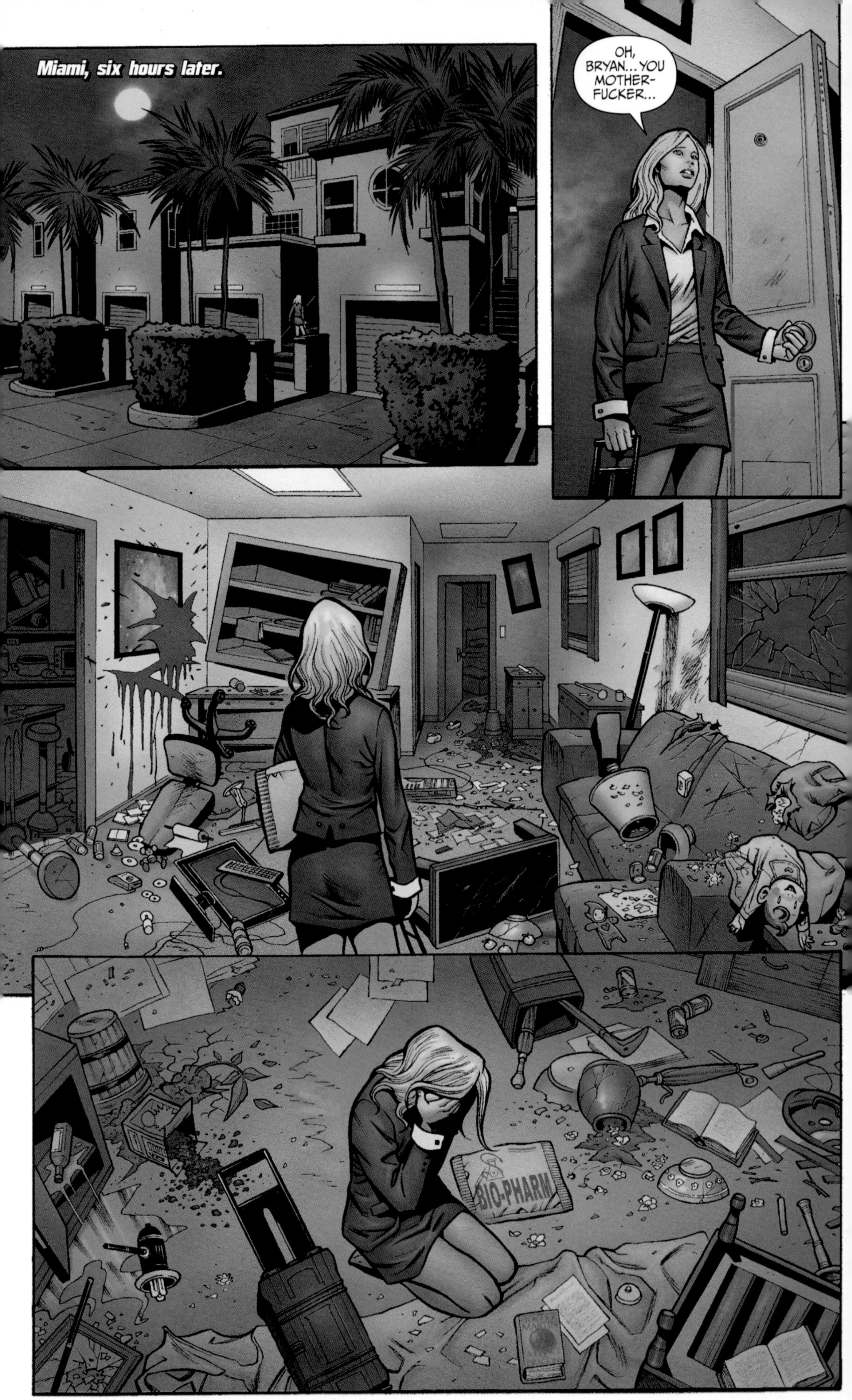
Miami, six hours later.
OH, BRYAN... YOU MOTHER-FUCKER...
BIO-PHARM

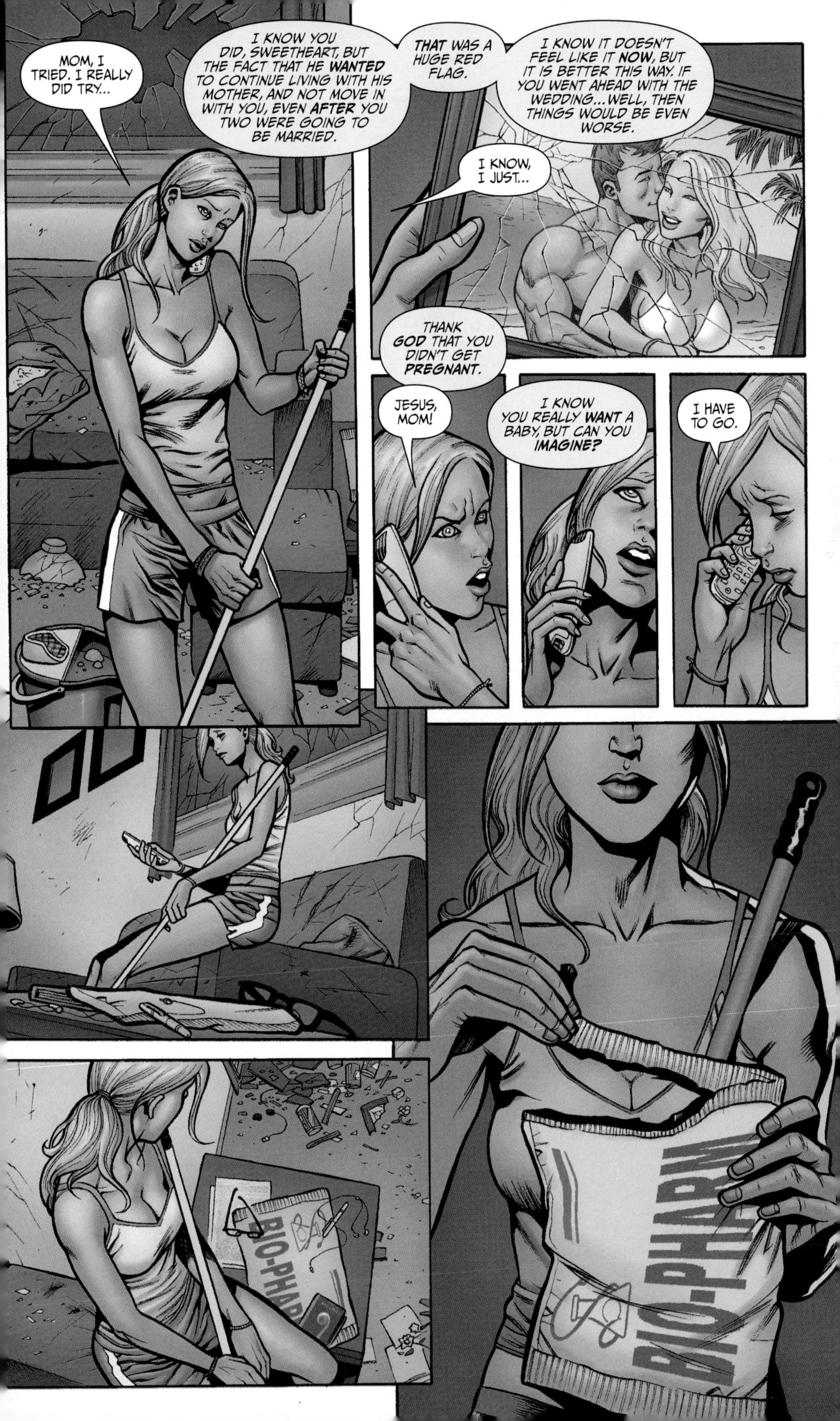
MOM, I TRIED. I REALLY DID TRY...
I KNOW YOU DID, SWEETHEART, BUT THE FACT THAT HE **WANTED** TO CONTINUE LIVING WITH HIS MOTHER, AND NOT MOVE IN WITH YOU, EVEN **AFTER** YOU TWO WERE GOING TO BE MARRIED.
THAT WAS A HUGE RED FLAG.
I KNOW IT DOESN'T FEEL LIKE IT **NOW**, BUT IT IS BETTER THIS WAY. IF YOU WENT AHEAD WITH THE WEDDING...WELL, THEN THINGS WOULD BE EVEN WORSE.
I KNOW, I JUST...
THANK **GOD** THAT YOU DIDN'T GET **PREGNANT**.
JESUS, MOM!
I KNOW YOU REALLY **WANT** A BABY, BUT CAN YOU **IMAGINE?**
I HAVE TO GO.
BIO-PHARM
BIO-PHARM

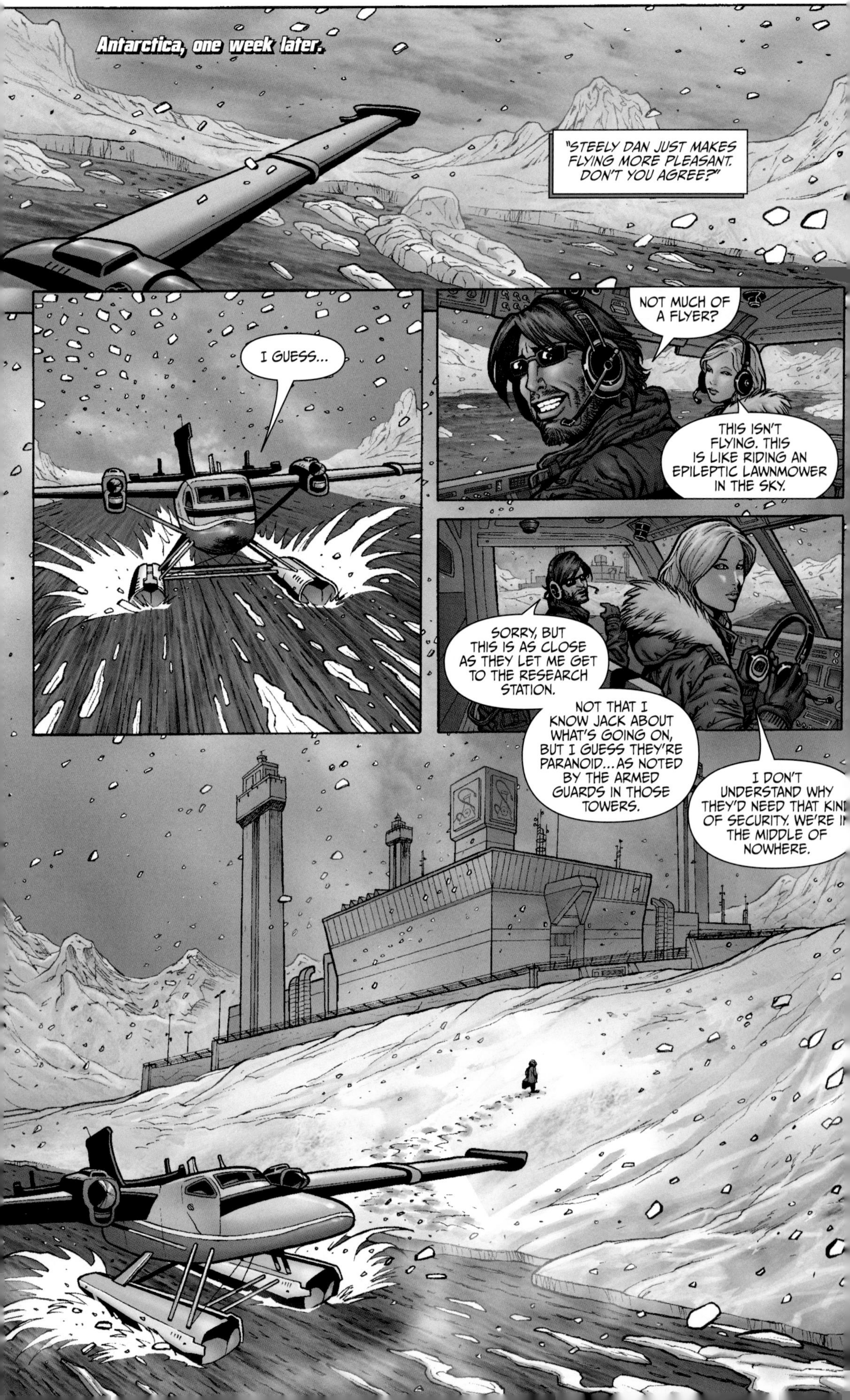
Antarctica, one week later.
"STEELY DAN JUST MAKES FLYING MORE PLEASANT. DON'T YOU AGREE?"
I GUESS...
NOT MUCH OF A FLYER?
THIS ISN'T FLYING. THIS IS LIKE RIDING AN EPILEPTIC LAWNMOWER IN THE SKY.
SORRY, BUT THIS IS AS CLOSE AS THEY LET ME GET TO THE RESEARCH STATION.
NOT THAT I KNOW JACK ABOUT WHAT'S GOING ON, BUT I GUESS THEY'RE PARANOID...AS NOTED BY THE ARMED GUARDS IN THOSE TOWERS.
I DON'T UNDERSTAND WHY THEY'D NEED THAT KIN OF SECURITY. WE'RE I THE MIDDLE OF NOWHERE.

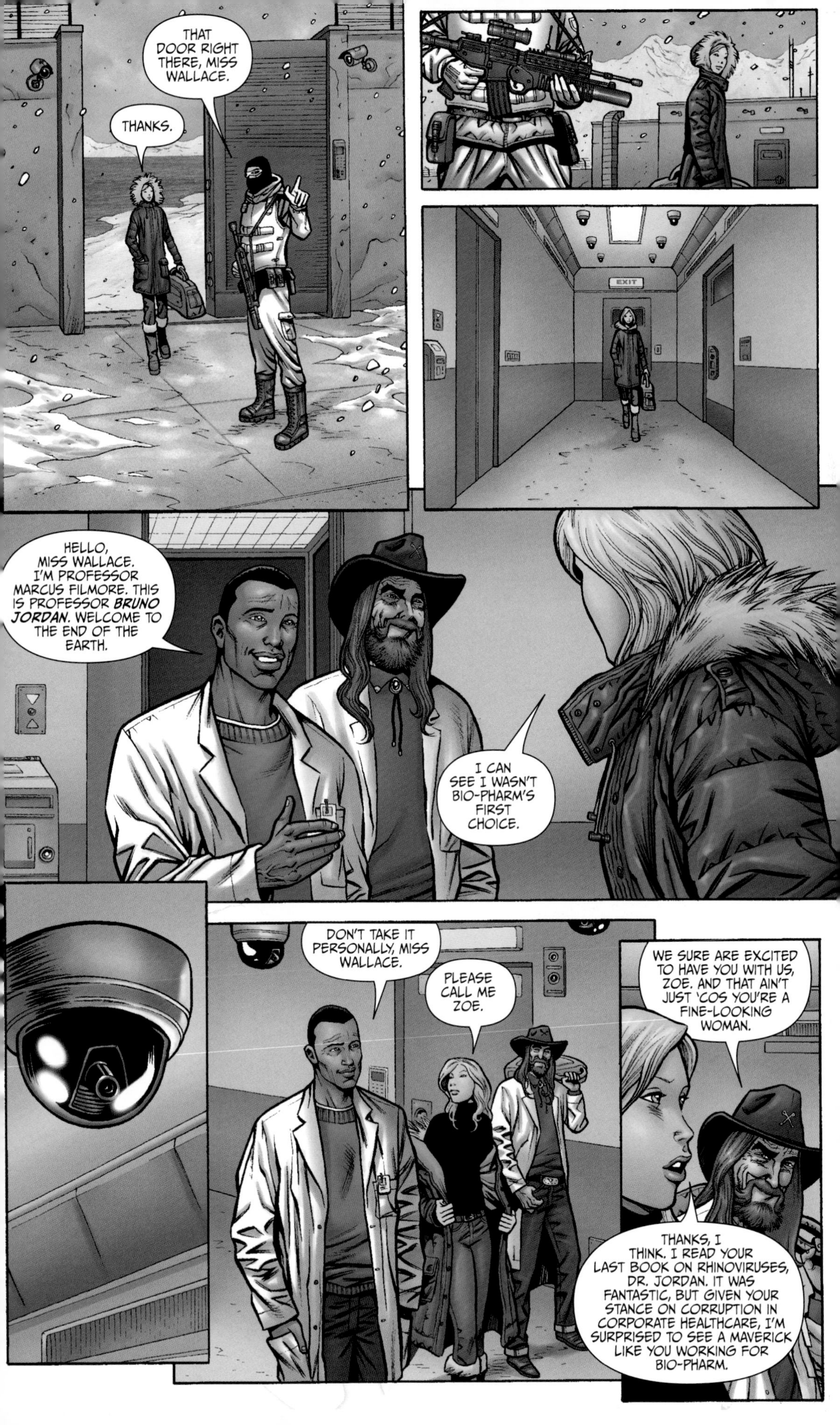
THAT DOOR RIGHT THERE, MISS WALLACE.
THANKS.
HELLO, MISS WALLACE. I'M PROFESSOR MARCUS FILMORE. THIS IS PROFESSOR BRUNO JORDAN. WELCOME TO THE END OF THE EARTH.
I CAN SEE I WASN'T BIO-PHARM'S FIRST CHOICE.
DON'T TAKE IT PERSONALLY, MISS WALLACE.
PLEASE CALL ME ZOE.
WE SURE ARE EXCITED TO HAVE YOU WITH US, ZOE. AND THAT AIN'T JUST 'COS YOU'RE A FINE-LOOKING WOMAN.
THANKS, I THINK. I READ YOUR LAST BOOK ON RHINOVIRUSES, DR. JORDAN. IT WAS FANTASTIC, BUT GIVEN YOUR STANCE ON CORRUPTION IN CORPORATE HEALTHCARE, I'M SURPRISED TO SEE A MAVERICK LIKE YOU WORKING FOR BIO-PHARM.

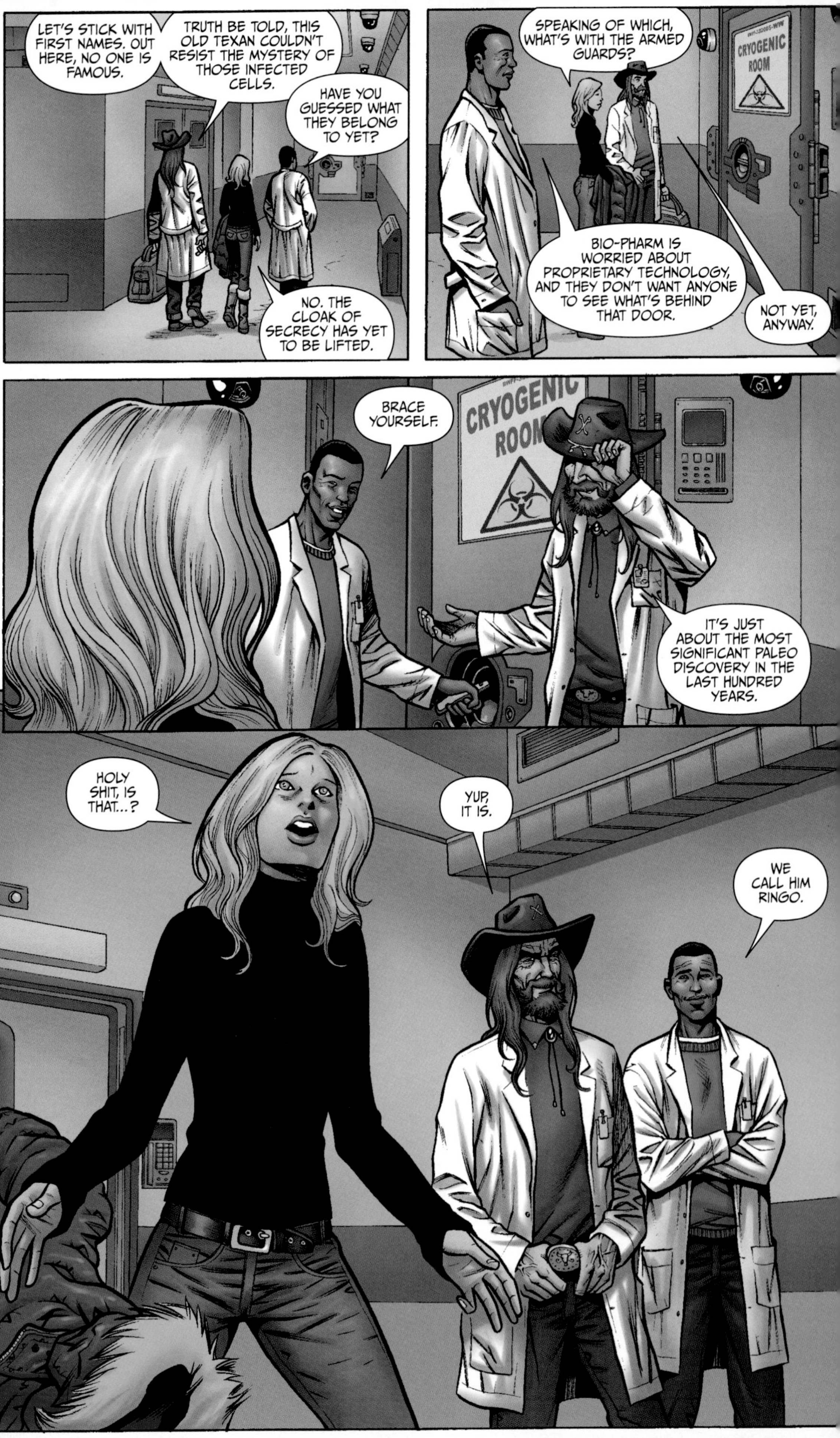

LET'S STICK WITH FIRST NAMES. OUT HERE, NO ONE IS FAMOUS.
TRUTH BE TOLD, THIS OLD TEXAN COULDN'T RESIST THE MYSTERY OF THOSE INFECTED CELLS.
HAVE YOU GUESSED WHAT THEY BELONG TO YET?
NO. THE CLOAK OF SECRECY HAS YET TO BE LIFTED.
SPEAKING OF WHICH, WHAT'S WITH THE ARMED GUARDS?
CRYOGENIC ROOM
BIO-PHARM IS WORRIED ABOUT PROPRIETARY TECHNOLOGY, AND THEY DON'T WANT ANYONE TO SEE WHAT'S BEHIND THAT DOOR.
NOT YET, ANYWAY.
BRACE YOURSELF.
CRYOGENIC ROOM
IT'S JUST ABOUT THE MOST SIGNIFICANT PALEO DISCOVERY IN THE LAST HUNDRED YEARS.
HOLY SHIT, IS THAT...?
YUP, IT IS.
WE CALL HIM RINGO.

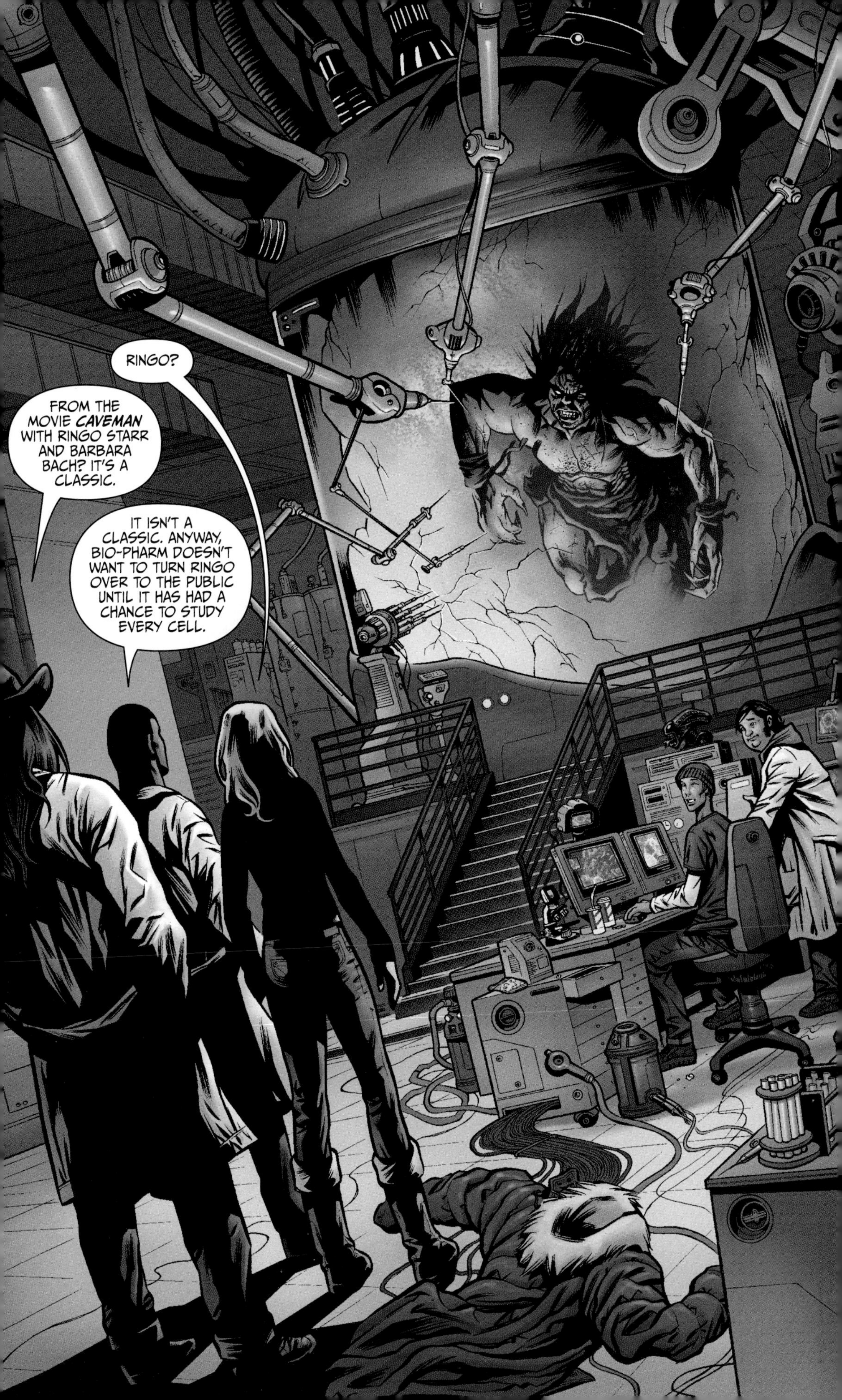
RINGO?
FROM THE MOVIE *CAVEMAN* WITH RINGO STARR AND BARBARA BACH? IT'S A CLASSIC.
IT ISN'T A CLASSIC. ANYWAY, BIO-PHARM DOESN'T WANT TO TURN RINGO OVER TO THE PUBLIC UNTIL IT HAS HAD A CHANCE TO STUDY EVERY CELL.

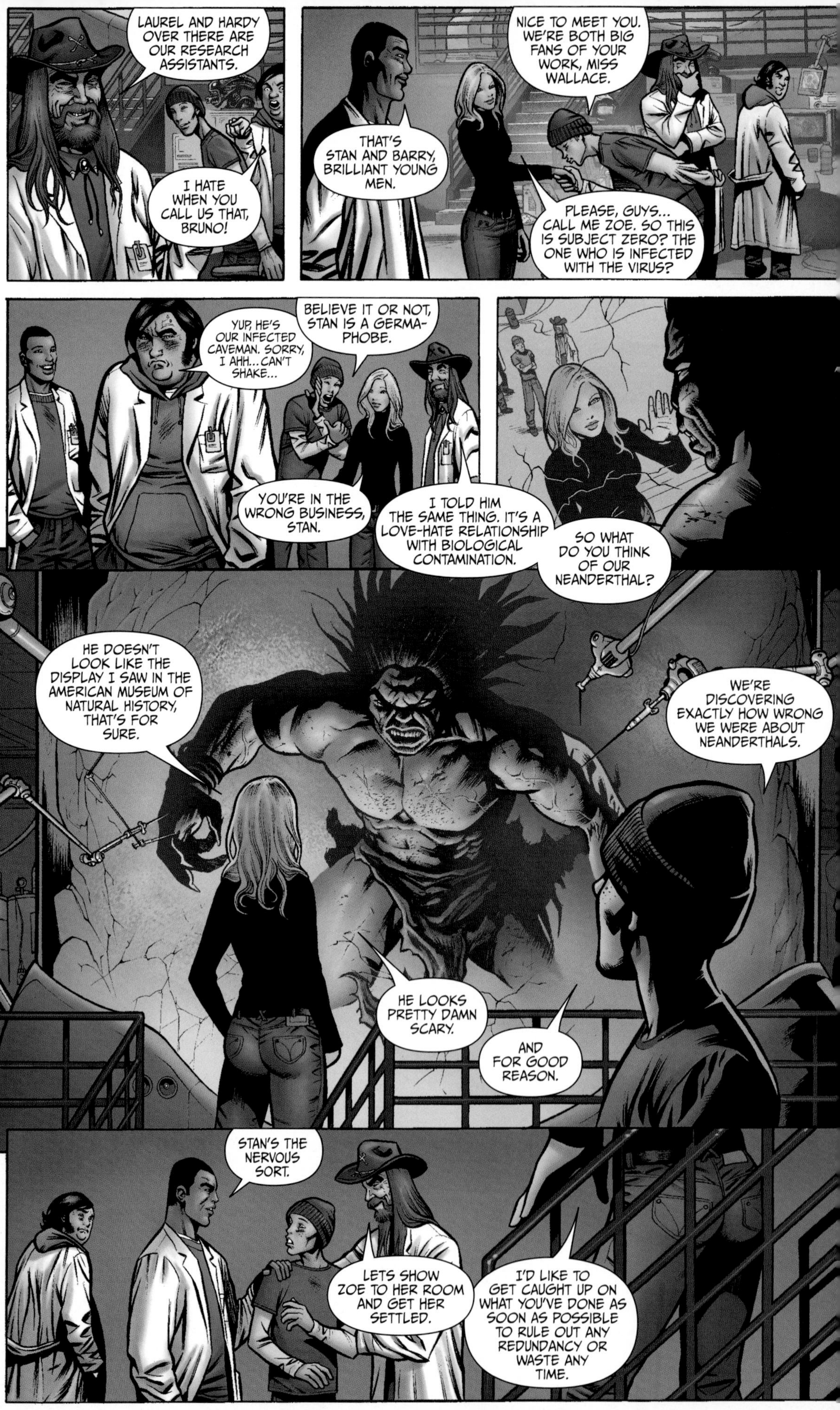
LAUREL AND HARDY OVER THERE ARE OUR RESEARCH ASSISTANTS.
I HATE WHEN YOU CALL US THAT, BRUNO!
NICE TO MEET YOU. WE'RE BOTH BIG FANS OF YOUR WORK, MISS WALLACE.
THAT'S STAN AND BARRY, BRILLIANT YOUNG MEN.
PLEASE, GUYS... CALL ME ZOE. SO THIS IS SUBJECT ZERO? THE ONE WHO IS INFECTED WITH THE VIRUS?
YUP, HE'S OUR INFECTED CAVEMAN. SORRY, I AHH...CAN'T SHAKE...
BELIEVE IT OR NOT, STAN IS A GERMA-PHOBE.
YOU'RE IN THE WRONG BUSINESS, STAN.
I TOLD HIM THE SAME THING. IT'S A LOVE-HATE RELATIONSHIP WITH BIOLOGICAL CONTAMINATION.
SO WHAT DO YOU THINK OF OUR NEANDERTHAL?
HE DOESN'T LOOK LIKE THE DISPLAY I SAW IN THE AMERICAN MUSEUM OF NATURAL HISTORY, THAT'S FOR SURE.
WE'RE DISCOVERING EXACTLY HOW WRONG WE WERE ABOUT NEANDERTHALS.
HE LOOKS PRETTY DAMN SCARY.
AND FOR GOOD REASON.
STAN'S THE NERVOUS SORT.
LETS SHOW ZOE TO HER ROOM AND GET HER SETTLED.
I'D LIKE TO GET CAUGHT UP ON WHAT YOU'VE DONE AS SOON AS POSSIBLE TO RULE OUT ANY REDUNDANCY OR WASTE ANY TIME.

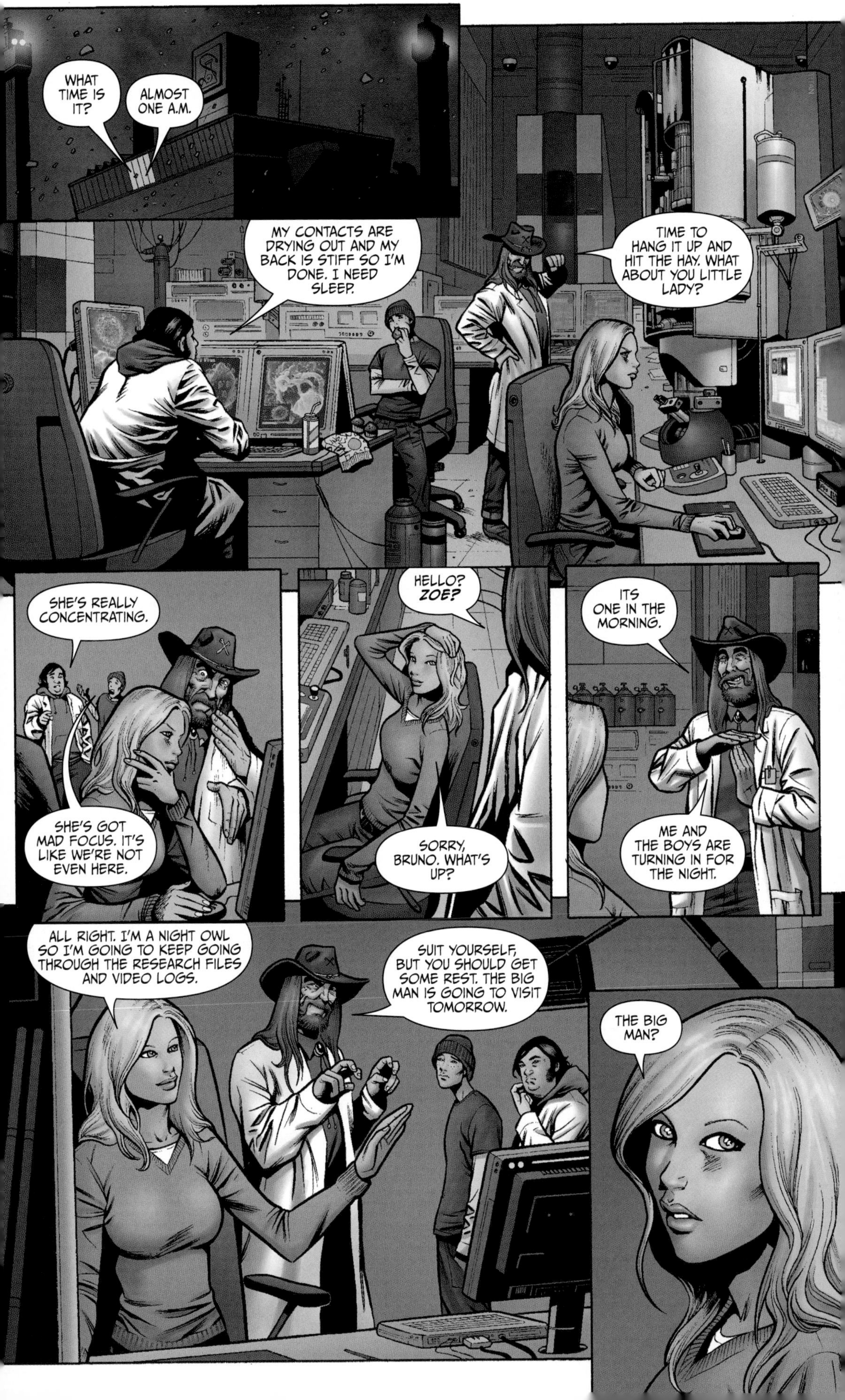
WHAT TIME IS IT?
ALMOST ONE A.M.
MY CONTACTS ARE DRYING OUT AND MY BACK IS STIFF SO I'M DONE. I NEED SLEEP.
TIME TO HANG IT UP AND HIT THE HAY. WHAT ABOUT YOU LITTLE LADY?
SHE'S REALLY CONCENTRATING.
SHE'S GOT MAD FOCUS. IT'S LIKE WE'RE NOT EVEN HERE.
HELLO? *ZOE?*
SORRY, BRUNO. WHAT'S UP?
ITS ONE IN THE MORNING.
ME AND THE BOYS ARE TURNING IN FOR THE NIGHT.
ALL RIGHT. I'M A NIGHT OWL SO I'M GOING TO KEEP GOING THROUGH THE RESEARCH FILES AND VIDEO LOGS.
SUIT YOURSELF, BUT YOU SHOULD GET SOME REST. THE BIG MAN IS GOING TO VISIT TOMORROW.
THE BIG MAN?

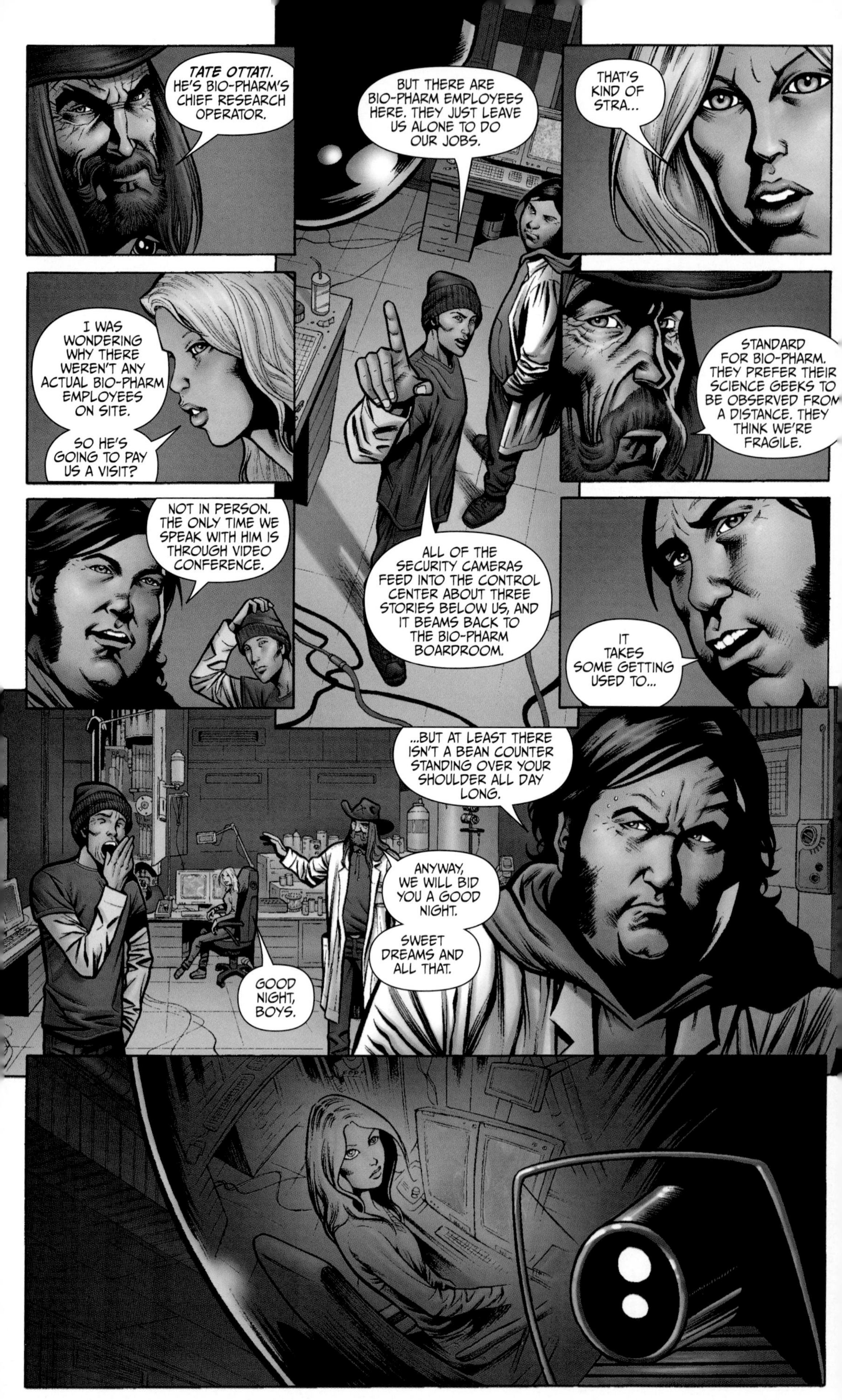
TATE OTTATI. HE'S BIO-PHARM'S CHIEF RESEARCH OPERATOR.
BUT THERE ARE BIO-PHARM EMPLOYEES HERE. THEY JUST LEAVE US ALONE TO DO OUR JOBS.
THAT'S KIND OF STRA...
I WAS WONDERING WHY THERE WEREN'T ANY ACTUAL BIO-PHARM EMPLOYEES ON SITE.
SO HE'S GOING TO PAY US A VISIT?
STANDARD FOR BIO-PHARM. THEY PREFER THEIR SCIENCE GEEKS TO BE OBSERVED FROM A DISTANCE. THEY THINK WE'RE FRAGILE.
NOT IN PERSON. THE ONLY TIME WE SPEAK WITH HIM IS THROUGH VIDEO CONFERENCE.
ALL OF THE SECURITY CAMERAS FEED INTO THE CONTROL CENTER ABOUT THREE STORIES BELOW US, AND IT BEAMS BACK TO THE BIO-PHARM BOARDROOM.
IT TAKES SOME GETTING USED TO...
...BUT AT LEAST THERE ISN'T A BEAN COUNTER STANDING OVER YOUR SHOULDER ALL DAY LONG.
ANYWAY, WE WILL BID YOU A GOOD NIGHT.
SWEET DREAMS AND ALL THAT.
GOOD NIGHT, BOYS.

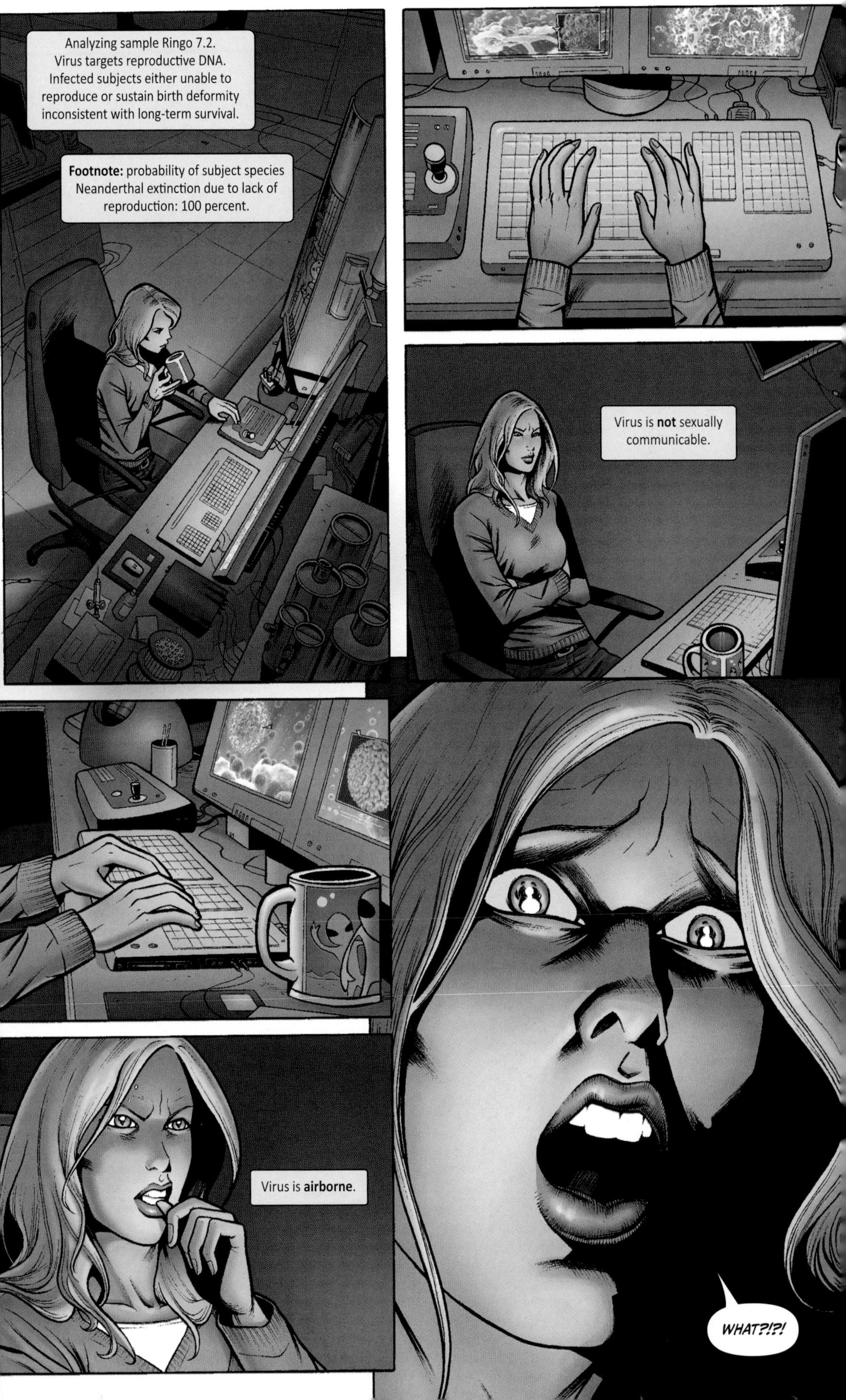
Analyzing sample Ringo 7.2.
Virus targets reproductive DNA.
Infected subjects either unable to reproduce or sustain birth deformity inconsistent with long-term survival.
Footnote: probability of subject species Neanderthal extinction due to lack of reproduction: 100 percent.
Virus is **not** sexually communicable.
Virus is **airborne**.
WHAT?!?!

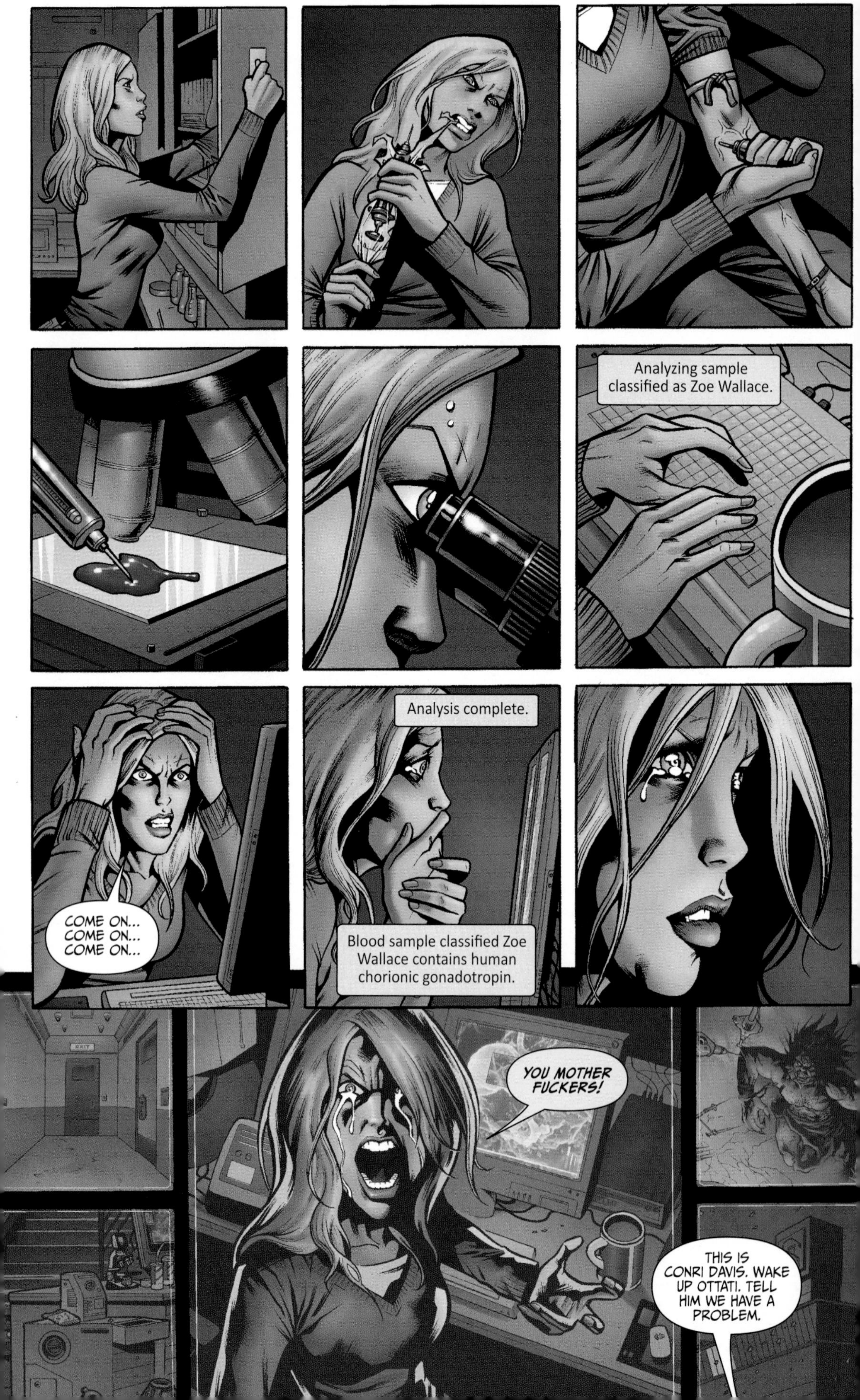
Analyzing sample classified as Zoe Wallace.
COME ON... COME ON... COME ON...
Analysis complete.
Blood sample classified Zoe Wallace contains human chorionic gonadotropin.
YOU MOTHER FUCKERS!
THIS IS CONRI DAVIS. WAKE UP OTTATI. TELL HIM WE HAVE A PROBLEM.

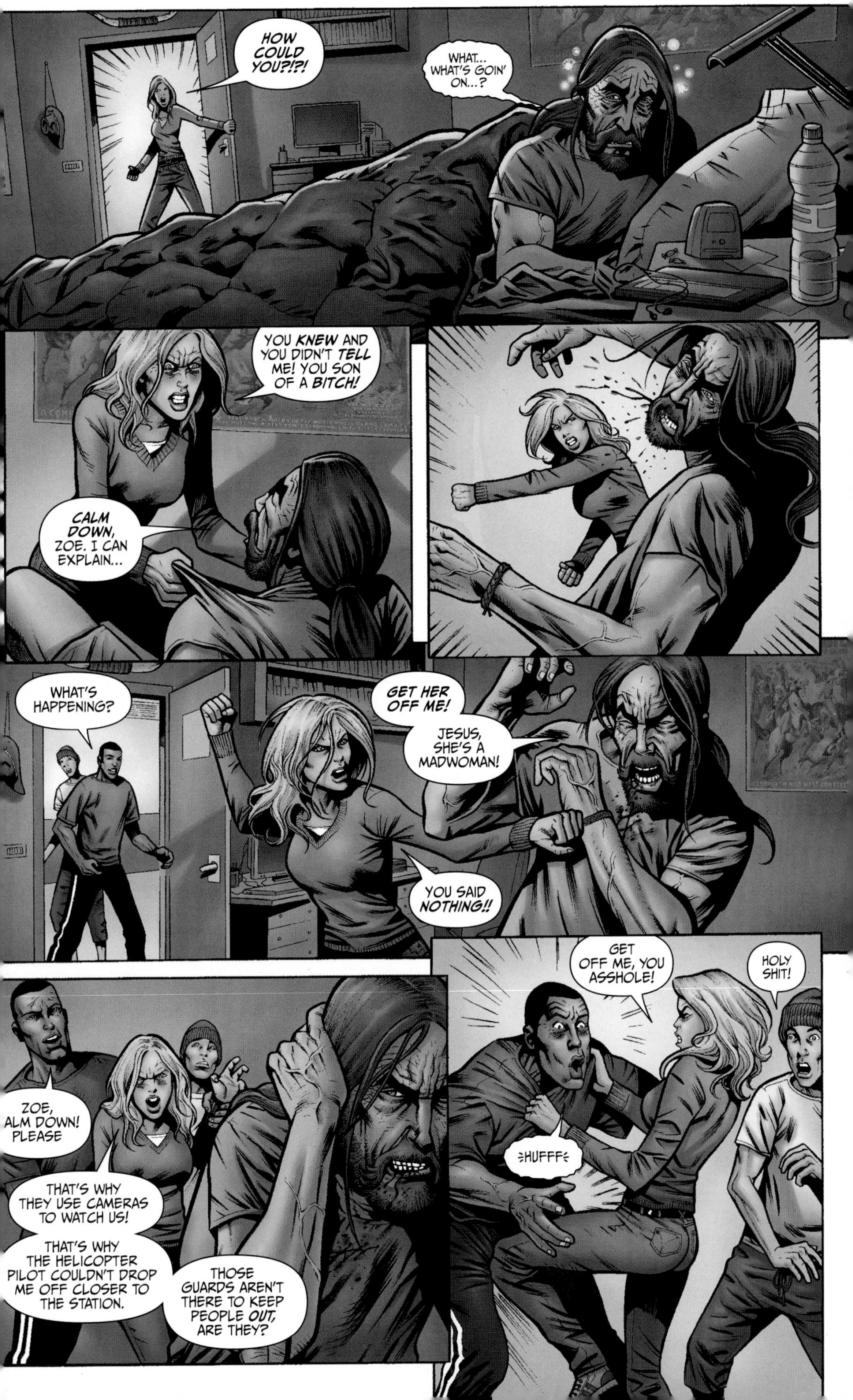
HOW COULD YOU?!?!
WHAT... WHAT'S GOIN' ON...?
YOU KNEW AND YOU DIDN'T TELL ME! YOU SON OF A BITCH!
CALM DOWN, ZOE. I CAN EXPLAIN...
WHAT'S HAPPENING?
GET HER OFF ME!
JESUS, SHE'S A MADWOMAN!
YOU SAID NOTHING!!
ZOE, ALM DOWN! PLEASE
THAT'S WHY THEY USE CAMERAS TO WATCH US!
THAT'S WHY THE HELICOPTER PILOT COULDN'T DROP ME OFF CLOSER TO THE STATION.
THOSE GUARDS AREN'T THERE TO KEEP PEOPLE OUT, ARE THEY?
GET OFF ME, YOU ASSHOLE!
HOLY SHIT!
≑HUFFF≑

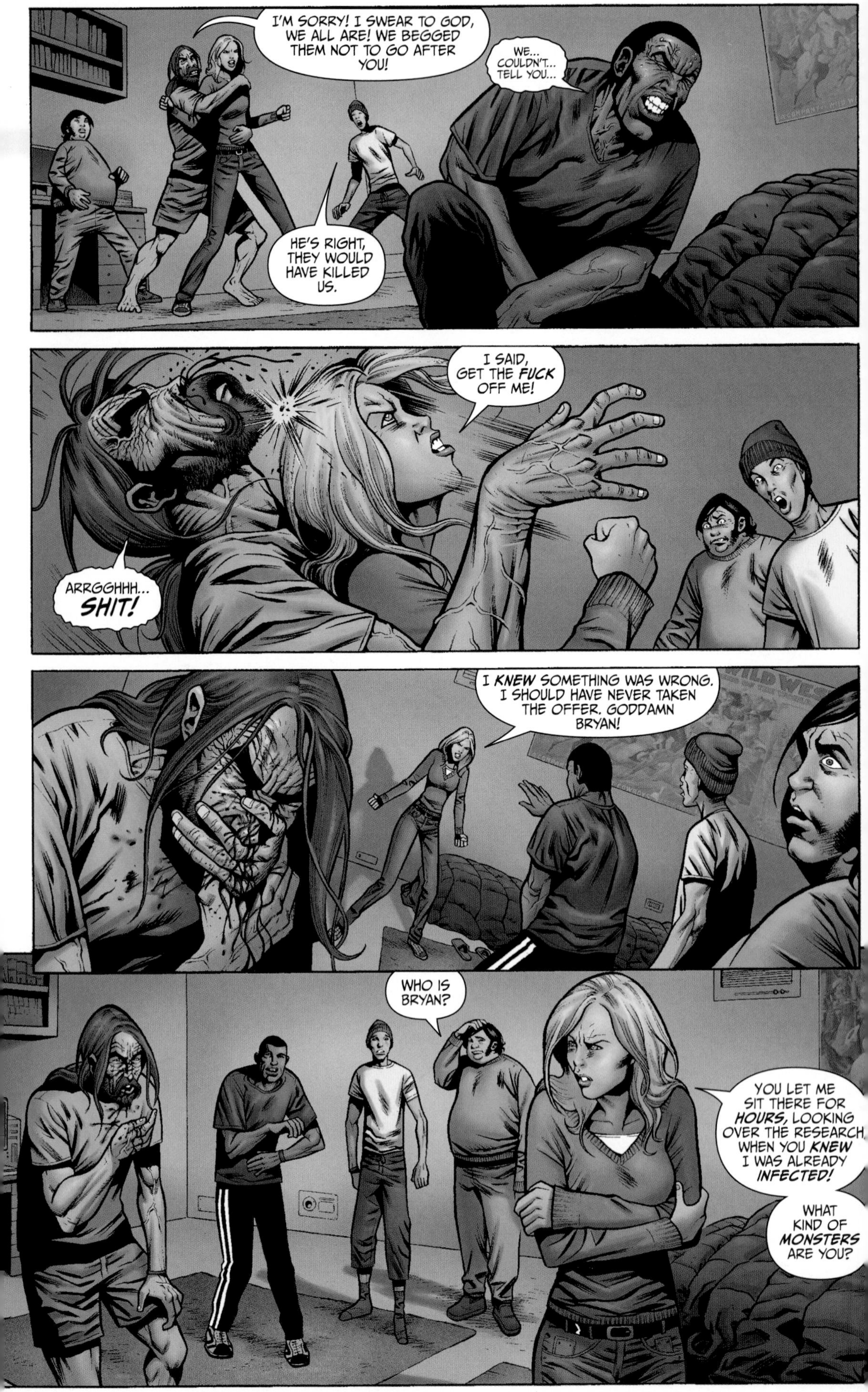

I'M SORRY! I SWEAR TO GOD, WE ALL ARE! WE BEGGED THEM NOT TO GO AFTER YOU!
WE... COULDN'T... TELL YOU...
HE'S RIGHT, THEY WOULD HAVE KILLED US.
I SAID, GET THE FUCK OFF ME!
ARRGGHHH... SHIT!
I KNEW SOMETHING WAS WRONG. I SHOULD HAVE NEVER TAKEN THE OFFER. GODDAMN BRYAN!
WHO IS BRYAN?
YOU LET ME SIT THERE FOR HOURS, LOOKING OVER THE RESEARCH WHEN YOU KNEW I WAS ALREADY INFECTED!
WHAT KIND OF MONSTERS ARE YOU?

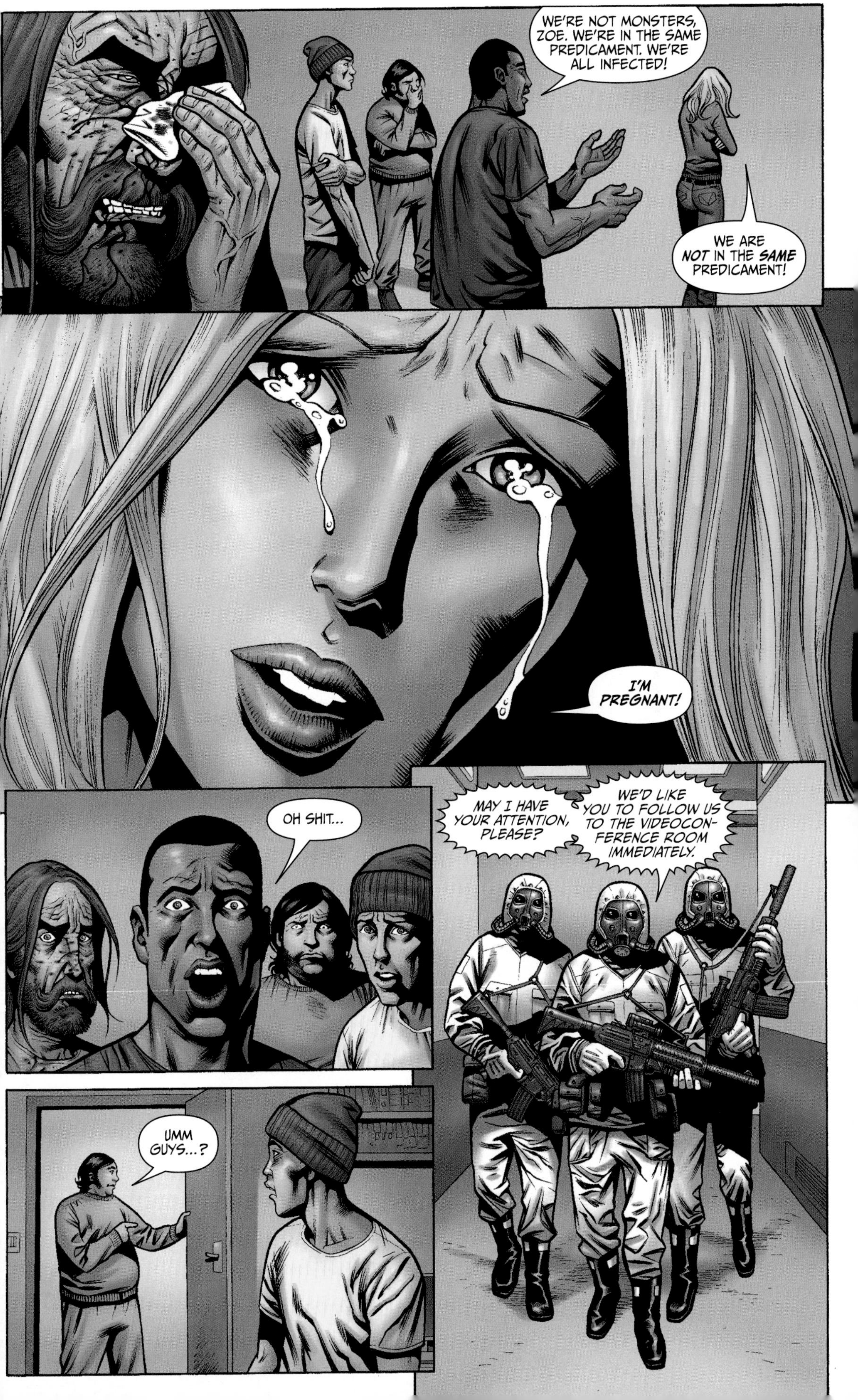

WE'RE NOT MONSTERS, ZOE. WE'RE IN THE SAME PREDICAMENT. WE'RE ALL INFECTED!
WE ARE *NOT* IN THE *SAME* PREDICAMENT!
I'M PREGNANT!
OH SHIT...
UMM GUYS...?
MAY I HAVE YOUR ATTENTION, PLEASE?
WE'D LIKE YOU TO FOLLOW US TO THE VIDEOCON-FERENCE ROOM IMMEDIATELY.

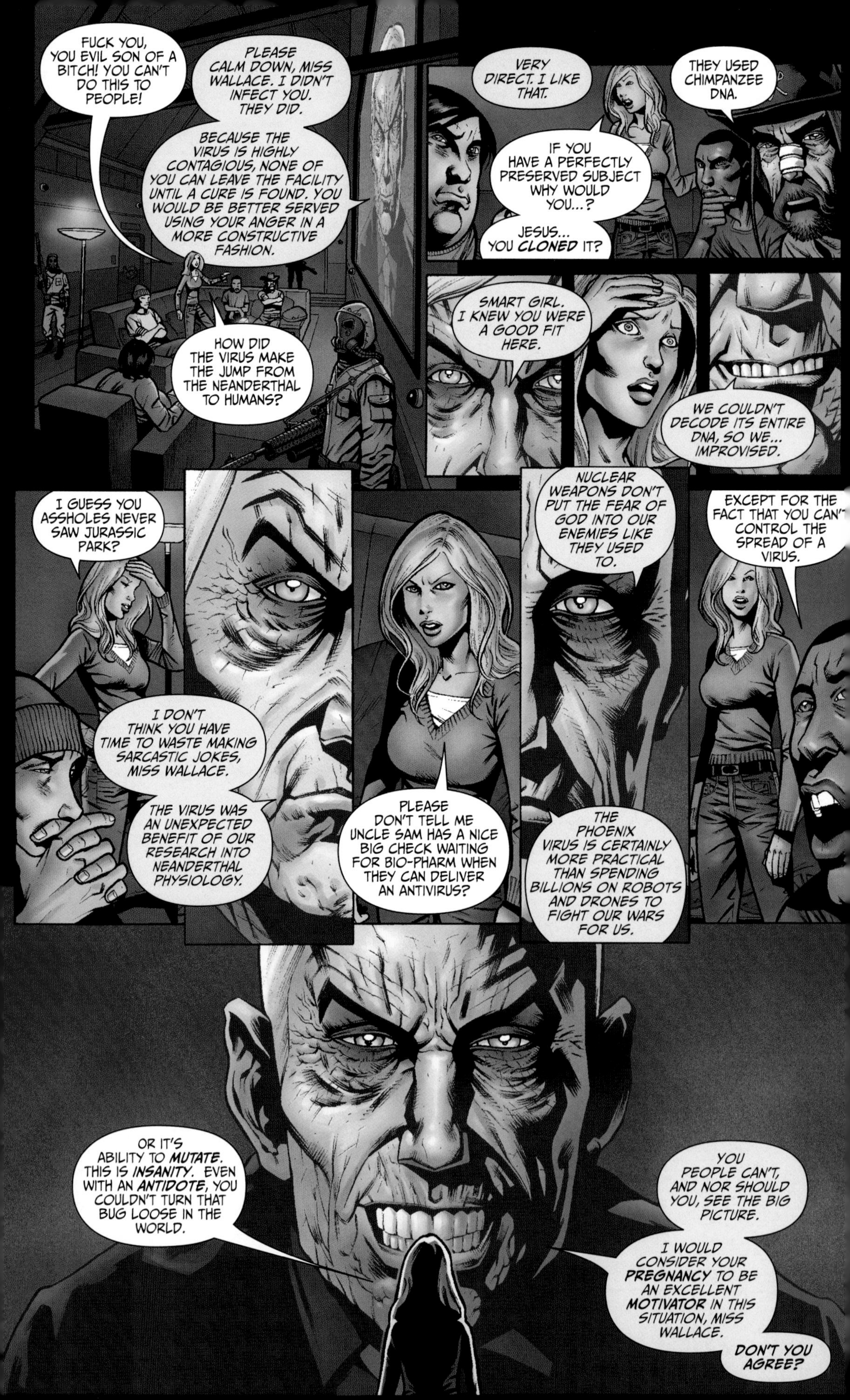
FUCK YOU, YOU EVIL SON OF A BITCH! YOU CAN'T DO THIS TO PEOPLE!
PLEASE CALM DOWN, MISS WALLACE. I DIDN'T INFECT YOU. THEY DID.
BECAUSE THE VIRUS IS HIGHLY CONTAGIOUS, NONE OF YOU CAN LEAVE THE FACILITY UNTIL A CURE IS FOUND. YOU WOULD BE BETTER SERVED USING YOUR ANGER IN A MORE CONSTRUCTIVE FASHION.
HOW DID THE VIRUS MAKE THE JUMP FROM THE NEANDERTHAL TO HUMANS?
VERY DIRECT. I LIKE THAT.
THEY USED CHIMPANZEE DNA.
IF YOU HAVE A PERFECTLY PRESERVED SUBJECT WHY WOULD YOU...?
JESUS... YOU CLONED IT?
SMART GIRL. I KNEW YOU WERE A GOOD FIT HERE.
WE COULDN'T DECODE ITS ENTIRE DNA, SO WE... IMPROVISED.
I GUESS YOU ASSHOLES NEVER SAW JURASSIC PARK?
I DON'T THINK YOU HAVE TIME TO WASTE MAKING SARCASTIC JOKES, MISS WALLACE.
THE VIRUS WAS AN UNEXPECTED BENEFIT OF OUR RESEARCH INTO NEANDERTHAL PHYSIOLOGY.
PLEASE DON'T TELL ME UNCLE SAM HAS A NICE BIG CHECK WAITING FOR BIO-PHARM WHEN THEY CAN DELIVER AN ANTIVIRUS?
NUCLEAR WEAPONS DON'T PUT THE FEAR OF GOD INTO OUR ENEMIES LIKE THEY USED TO.
THE PHOENIX VIRUS IS CERTAINLY MORE PRACTICAL THAN SPENDING BILLIONS ON ROBOTS AND DRONES TO FIGHT OUR WARS FOR US.
EXCEPT FOR THE FACT THAT YOU CAN'T CONTROL THE SPREAD OF A VIRUS.
OR IT'S ABILITY TO MUTATE. THIS IS INSANITY. EVEN WITH AN ANTIDOTE, YOU COULDN'T TURN THAT BUG LOOSE IN THE WORLD.
YOU PEOPLE CAN'T, AND NOR SHOULD YOU, SEE THE BIG PICTURE.
I WOULD CONSIDER YOUR PREGNANCY TO BE AN EXCELLENT MOTIVATOR IN THIS SITUATION, MISS WALLACE.
DON'T YOU AGREE?

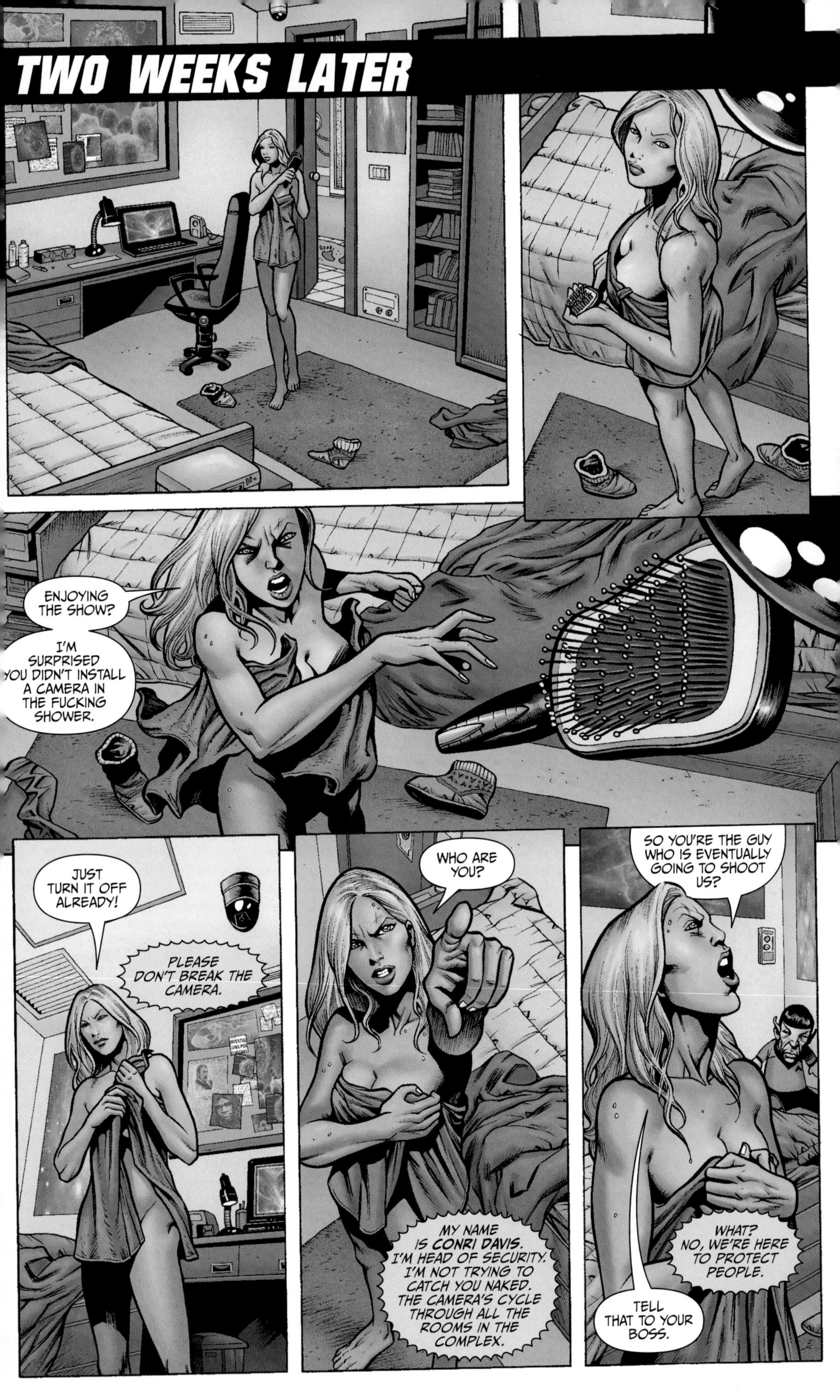
TWO WEEKS LATER
ENJOYING THE SHOW?
I'M SURPRISED YOU DIDN'T INSTALL A CAMERA IN THE FUCKING SHOWER.
JUST TURN IT OFF ALREADY!
PLEASE DON'T BREAK THE CAMERA.
WHO ARE YOU?
MY NAME IS CONRI DAVIS. I'M HEAD OF SECURITY. I'M NOT TRYING TO CATCH YOU NAKED. THE CAMERA'S CYCLE THROUGH ALL THE ROOMS IN THE COMPLEX.
SO YOU'RE THE GUY WHO IS EVENTUALLY GOING TO SHOOT US?
WHAT? NO, WE'RE HERE TO PROTECT PEOPLE.
TELL THAT TO YOUR BOSS.

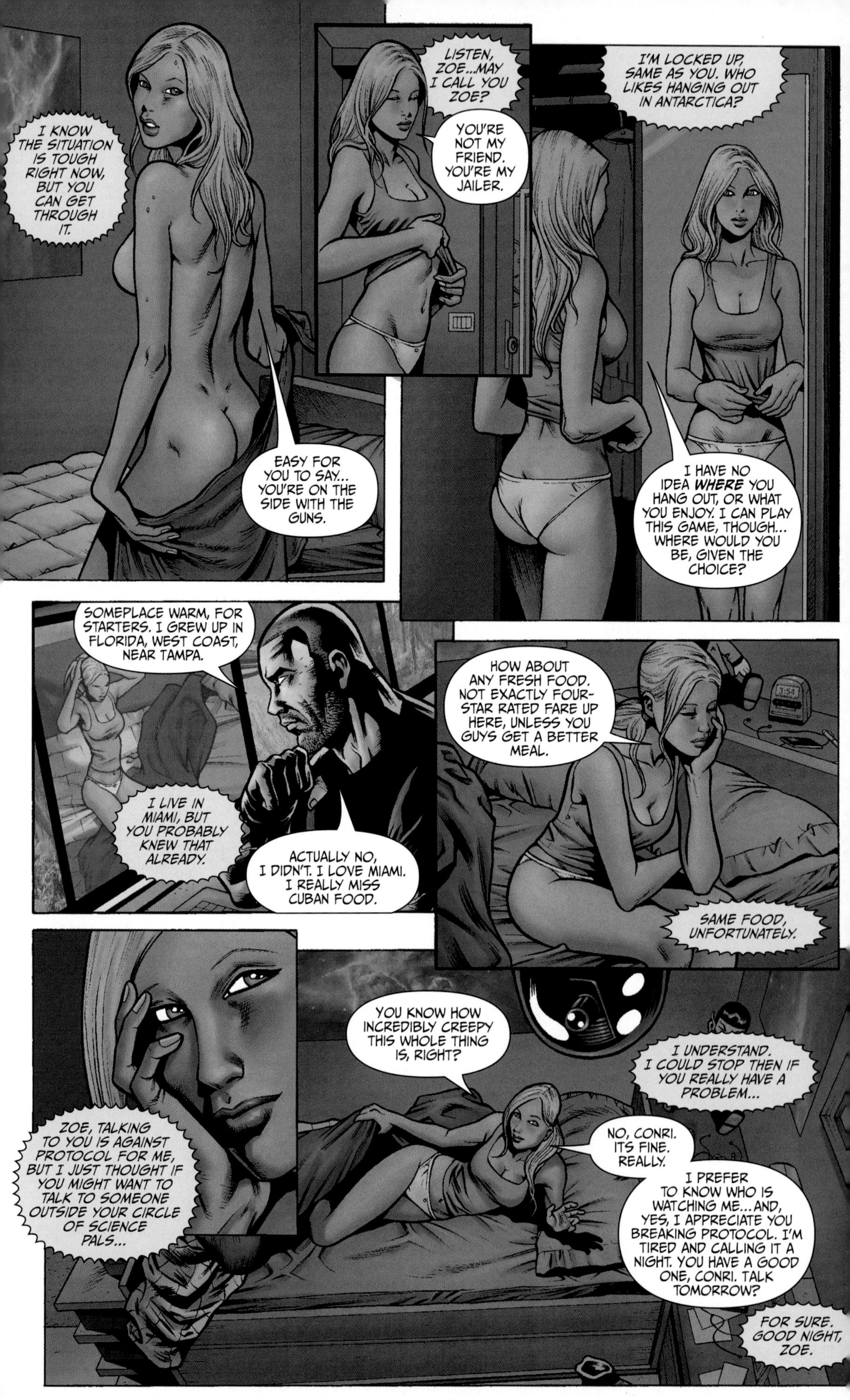
I KNOW THE SITUATION IS TOUGH RIGHT NOW, BUT YOU CAN GET THROUGH IT.
EASY FOR YOU TO SAY... YOU'RE ON THE SIDE WITH THE GUNS.
LISTEN, ZOE...MAY I CALL YOU ZOE?
YOU'RE NOT MY FRIEND. YOU'RE MY JAILER.
I'M LOCKED UP, SAME AS YOU. WHO LIKES HANGING OUT IN ANTARCTICA?
I HAVE NO IDEA **WHERE** YOU HANG OUT, OR WHAT YOU ENJOY. I CAN PLAY THIS GAME, THOUGH... WHERE WOULD YOU BE, GIVEN THE CHOICE?
SOMEPLACE WARM, FOR STARTERS. I GREW UP IN FLORIDA, WEST COAST, NEAR TAMPA.
I LIVE IN MIAMI, BUT YOU PROBABLY KNEW THAT ALREADY.
ACTUALLY NO, I DIDN'T. I LOVE MIAMI. I REALLY MISS CUBAN FOOD.
HOW ABOUT ANY FRESH FOOD. NOT EXACTLY FOUR-STAR RATED FARE UP HERE, UNLESS YOU GUYS GET A BETTER MEAL.
SAME FOOD, UNFORTUNATELY.
ZOE, TALKING TO YOU IS AGAINST PROTOCOL FOR ME, BUT I JUST THOUGHT IF YOU MIGHT WANT TO TALK TO SOMEONE OUTSIDE YOUR CIRCLE OF SCIENCE PALS...
YOU KNOW HOW INCREDIBLY CREEPY THIS WHOLE THING IS, RIGHT?
I UNDERSTAND. I COULD STOP THEN IF YOU REALLY HAVE A PROBLEM...
NO, CONRI. ITS FINE. REALLY.
I PREFER TO KNOW WHO IS WATCHING ME...AND, YES, I APPRECIATE YOU BREAKING PROTOCOL. I'M TIRED AND CALLING IT A NIGHT. YOU HAVE A GOOD ONE, CONRI. TALK TOMORROW?
FOR SURE. GOOD NIGHT, ZOE.

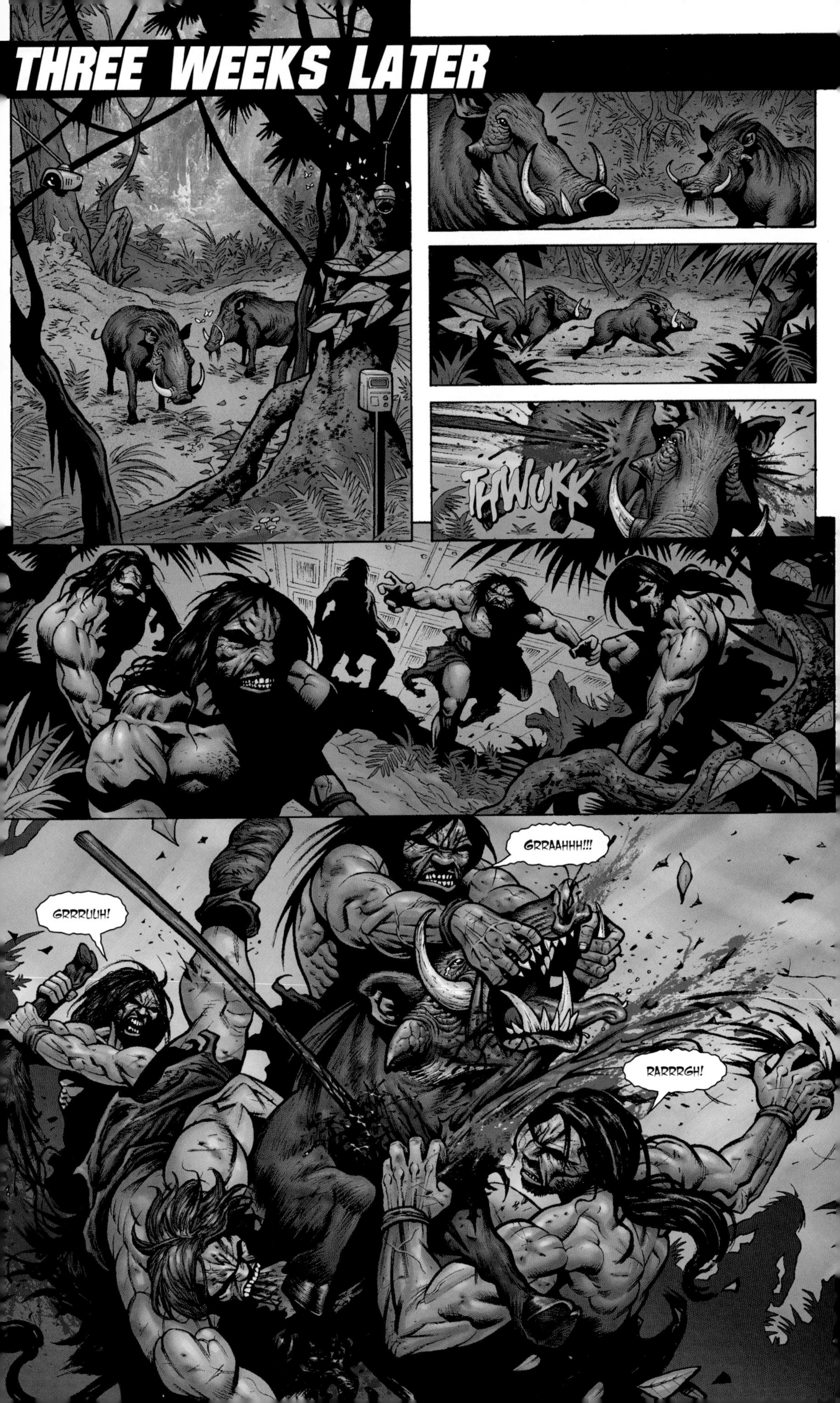
THREE WEEKS LATER
THWUKK
GRRAAHHH!!!
GRRRUUH!
RARRRGH!

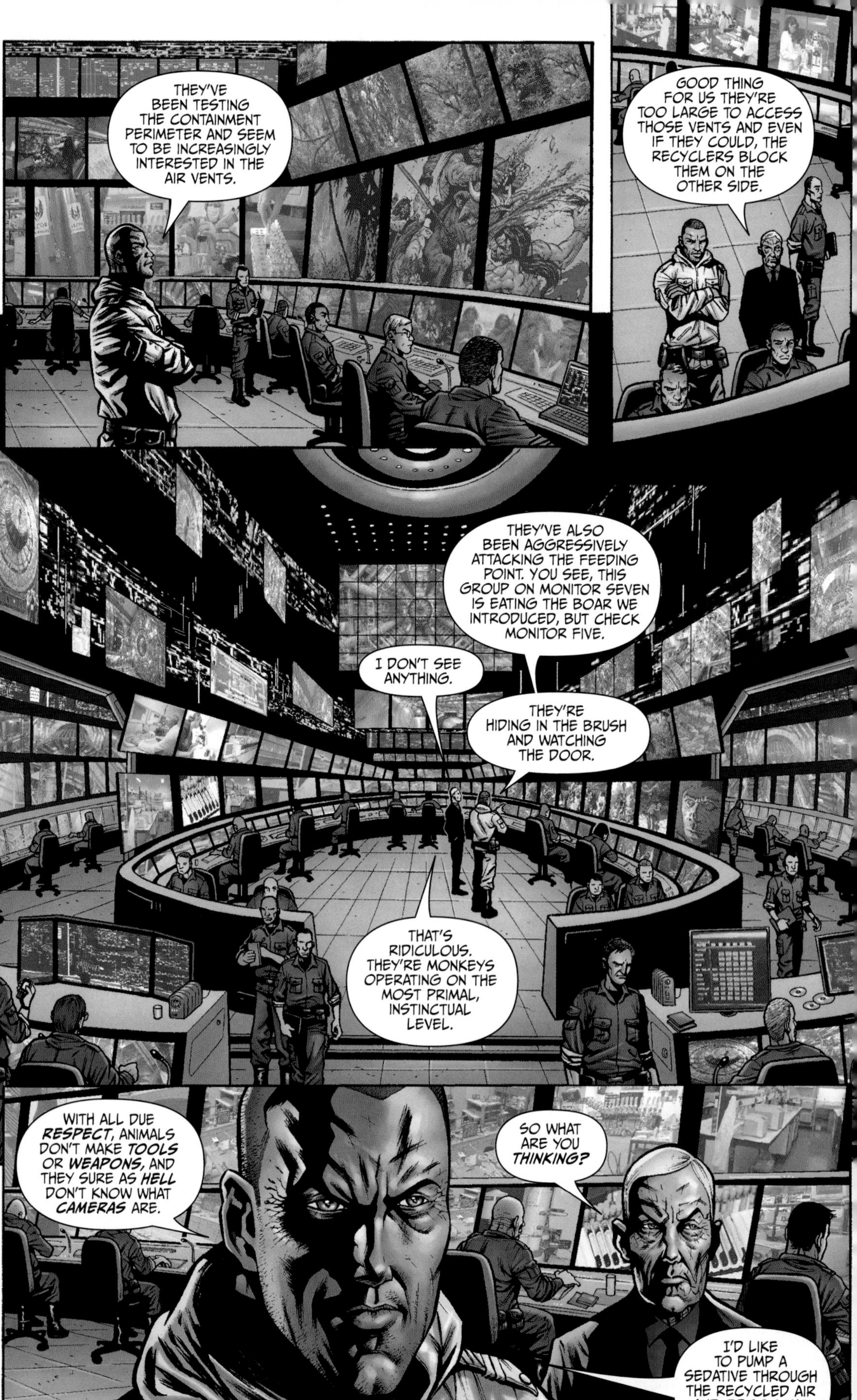

THEY'VE BEEN TESTING THE CONTAINMENT PERIMETER AND SEEM TO BE INCREASINGLY INTERESTED IN THE AIR VENTS.
GOOD THING FOR US THEY'RE TOO LARGE TO ACCESS THOSE VENTS AND EVEN IF THEY COULD, THE RECYCLERS BLOCK THEM ON THE OTHER SIDE.
THEY'VE ALSO BEEN AGGRESSIVELY ATTACKING THE FEEDING POINT. YOU SEE, THIS GROUP ON MONITOR SEVEN IS EATING THE BOAR WE INTRODUCED, BUT CHECK MONITOR FIVE.
I DON'T SEE ANYTHING.
THEY'RE HIDING IN THE BRUSH AND WATCHING THE DOOR.
THAT'S RIDICULOUS. THEY'RE MONKEYS OPERATING ON THE MOST PRIMAL, INSTINCTUAL LEVEL.
WITH ALL DUE RESPECT, ANIMALS DON'T MAKE TOOLS OR WEAPONS, AND THEY SURE AS HELL DON'T KNOW WHAT CAMERAS ARE.
SO WHAT ARE YOU THINKING?
I'D LIKE TO PUMP A SEDATIVE THROUGH THE RECYCLED AIR AND RECON THE ENVIRONMENT.

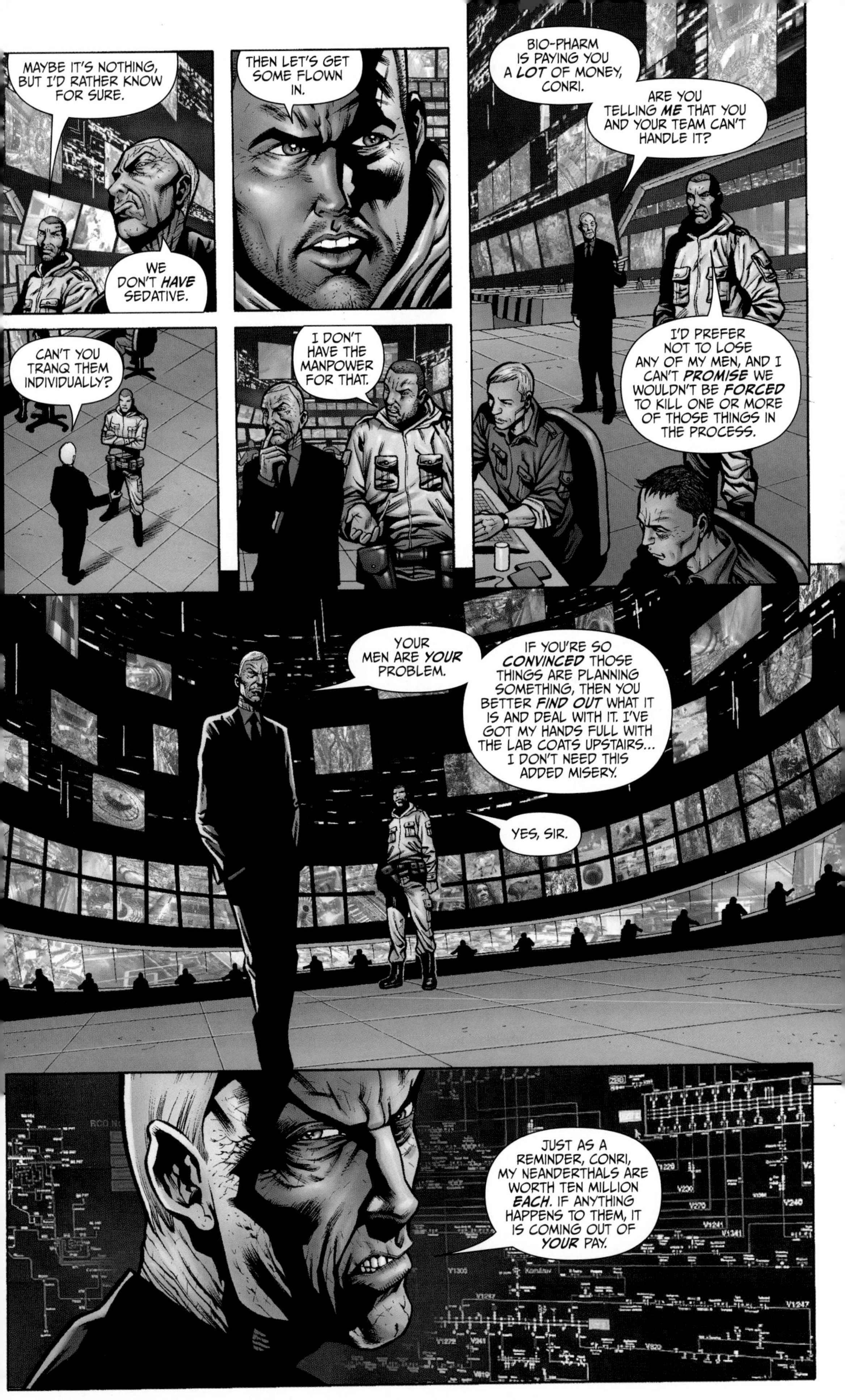

MAYBE IT'S NOTHING, BUT I'D RATHER KNOW FOR SURE.
WE DON'T *HAVE* SEDATIVE.
THEN LET'S GET SOME FLOWN IN.
BIO-PHARM IS PAYING YOU A *LOT* OF MONEY, CONRI.
ARE YOU TELLING *ME* THAT YOU AND YOUR TEAM CAN'T HANDLE IT?
CAN'T YOU TRANQ THEM INDIVIDUALLY?
I DON'T HAVE THE MANPOWER FOR THAT.
I'D PREFER NOT TO LOSE ANY OF MY MEN, AND I CAN'T *PROMISE* WE WOULDN'T BE *FORCED* TO KILL ONE OR MORE OF THOSE THINGS IN THE PROCESS.
YOUR MEN ARE *YOUR* PROBLEM.
IF YOU'RE SO *CONVINCED* THOSE THINGS ARE PLANNING SOMETHING, THEN YOU BETTER *FIND OUT* WHAT IT IS AND DEAL WITH IT. I'VE GOT MY HANDS FULL WITH THE LAB COATS UPSTAIRS... I DON'T NEED THIS ADDED MISERY.
YES, SIR.
JUST AS A REMINDER, CONRI, MY NEANDERTHALS ARE WORTH TEN MILLION *EACH*. IF ANYTHING HAPPENS TO THEM, IT IS COMING OUT OF *YOUR* PAY.

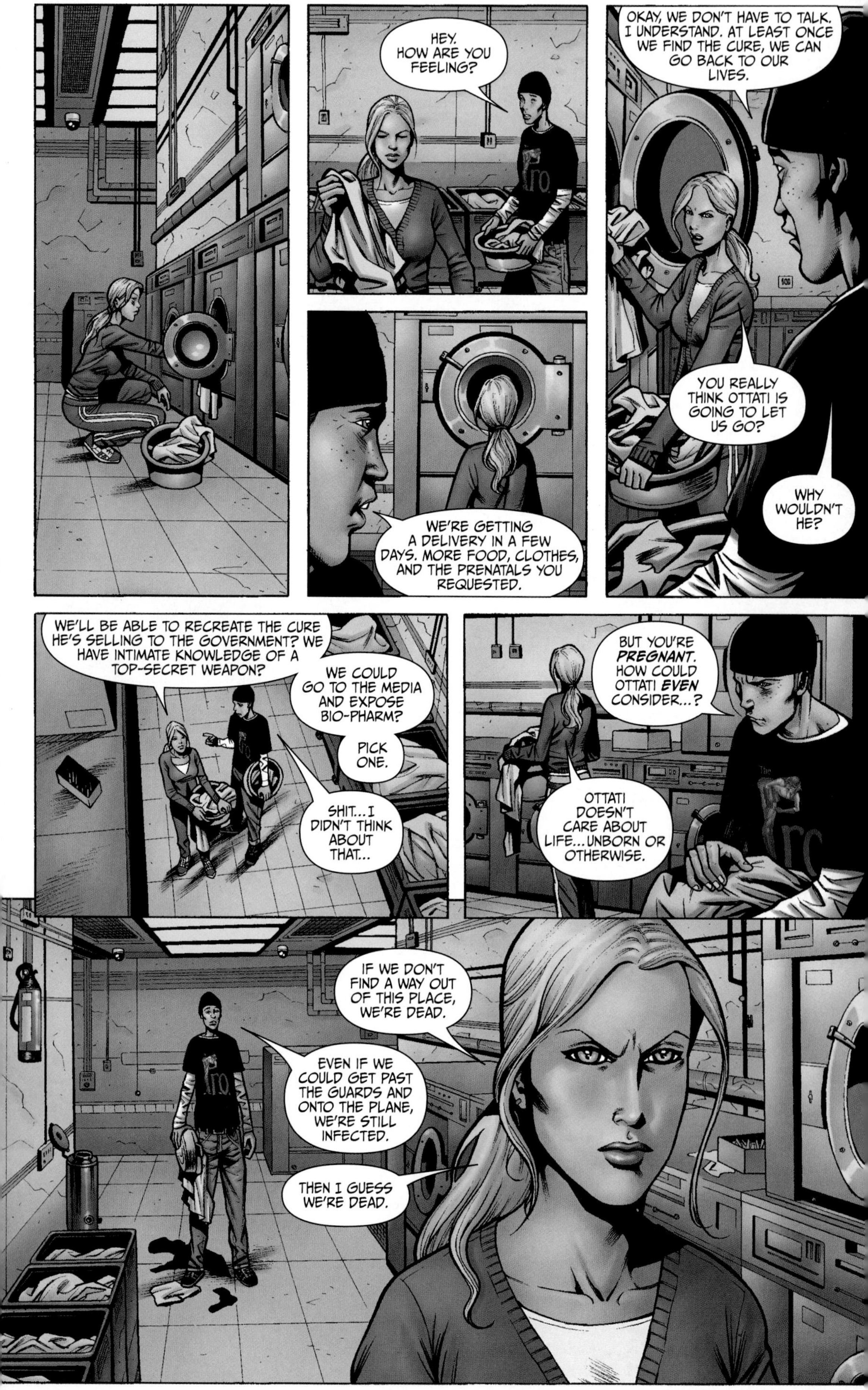
HEY. HOW ARE YOU FEELING?
OKAY, WE DON'T HAVE TO TALK. I UNDERSTAND. AT LEAST ONCE WE FIND THE CURE, WE CAN GO BACK TO OUR LIVES.
WE'RE GETTING A DELIVERY IN A FEW DAYS. MORE FOOD, CLOTHES, AND THE PRENATALS YOU REQUESTED.
YOU REALLY THINK OTTATI IS GOING TO LET US GO?
WHY WOULDN'T HE?
WE'LL BE ABLE TO RECREATE THE CURE HE'S SELLING TO THE GOVERNMENT? WE HAVE INTIMATE KNOWLEDGE OF A TOP-SECRET WEAPON?
WE COULD GO TO THE MEDIA AND EXPOSE BIO-PHARM?
PICK ONE.
SHIT...I DIDN'T THINK ABOUT THAT...
BUT YOU'RE PREGNANT. HOW COULD OTTATI EVEN CONSIDER...?
OTTATI DOESN'T CARE ABOUT LIFE...UNBORN OR OTHERWISE.
IF WE DON'T FIND A WAY OUT OF THIS PLACE, WE'RE DEAD.
EVEN IF WE COULD GET PAST THE GUARDS AND ONTO THE PLANE, WE'RE STILL INFECTED.
THEN I GUESS WE'RE DEAD.

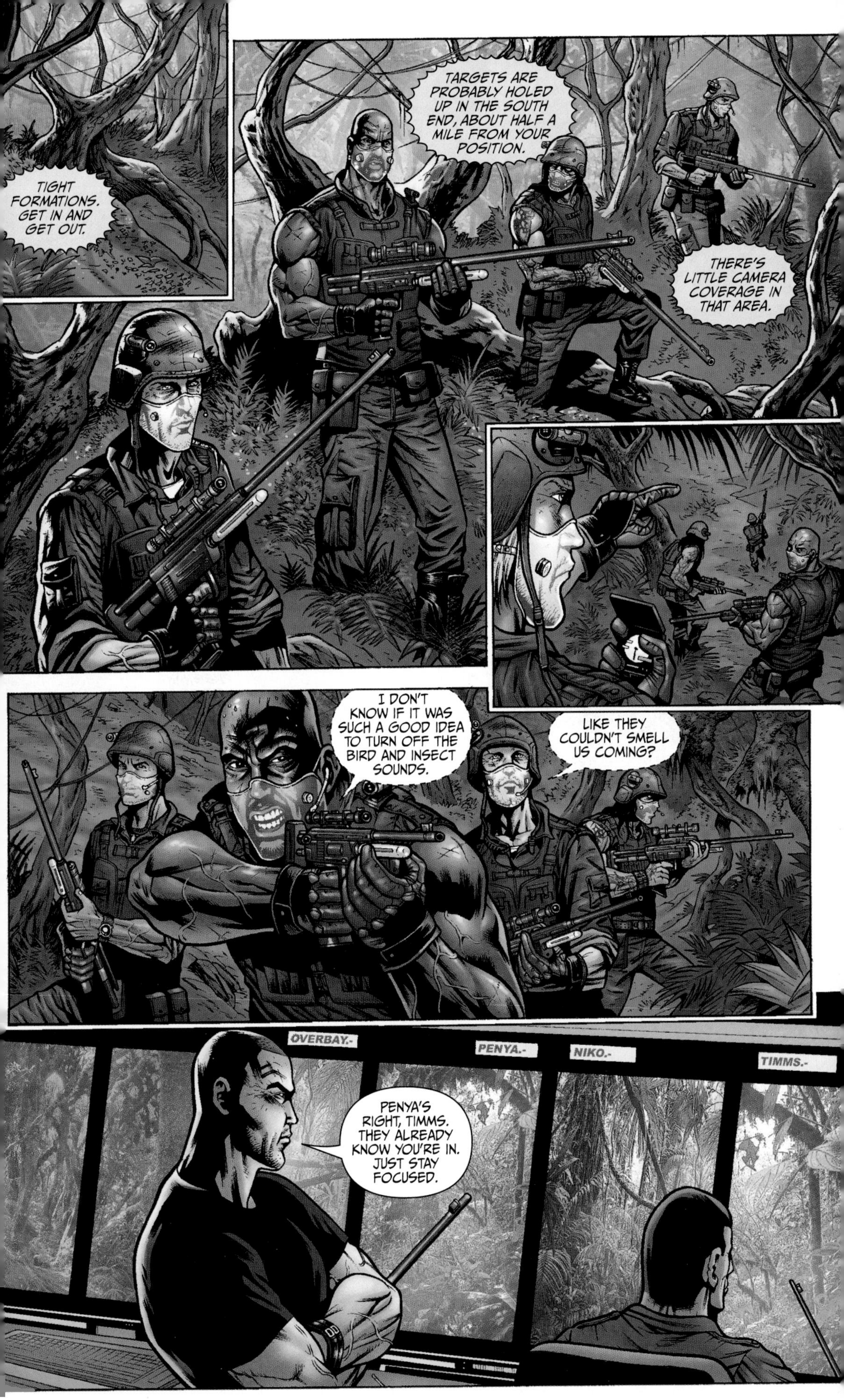
TIGHT FORMATIONS. GET IN AND GET OUT.
TARGETS ARE PROBABLY HOLED UP IN THE SOUTH END, ABOUT HALF A MILE FROM YOUR POSITION.
THERE'S LITTLE CAMERA COVERAGE IN THAT AREA.
I DON'T KNOW IF IT WAS SUCH A GOOD IDEA TO TURN OFF THE BIRD AND INSECT SOUNDS.
LIKE THEY COULDN'T SMELL US COMING?
OVERBAY.-
PENYA.-
NIKO.-
TIMMS.-
PENYA'S RIGHT, TIMMS. THEY ALREADY KNOW YOU'RE IN. JUST STAY FOCUSED.

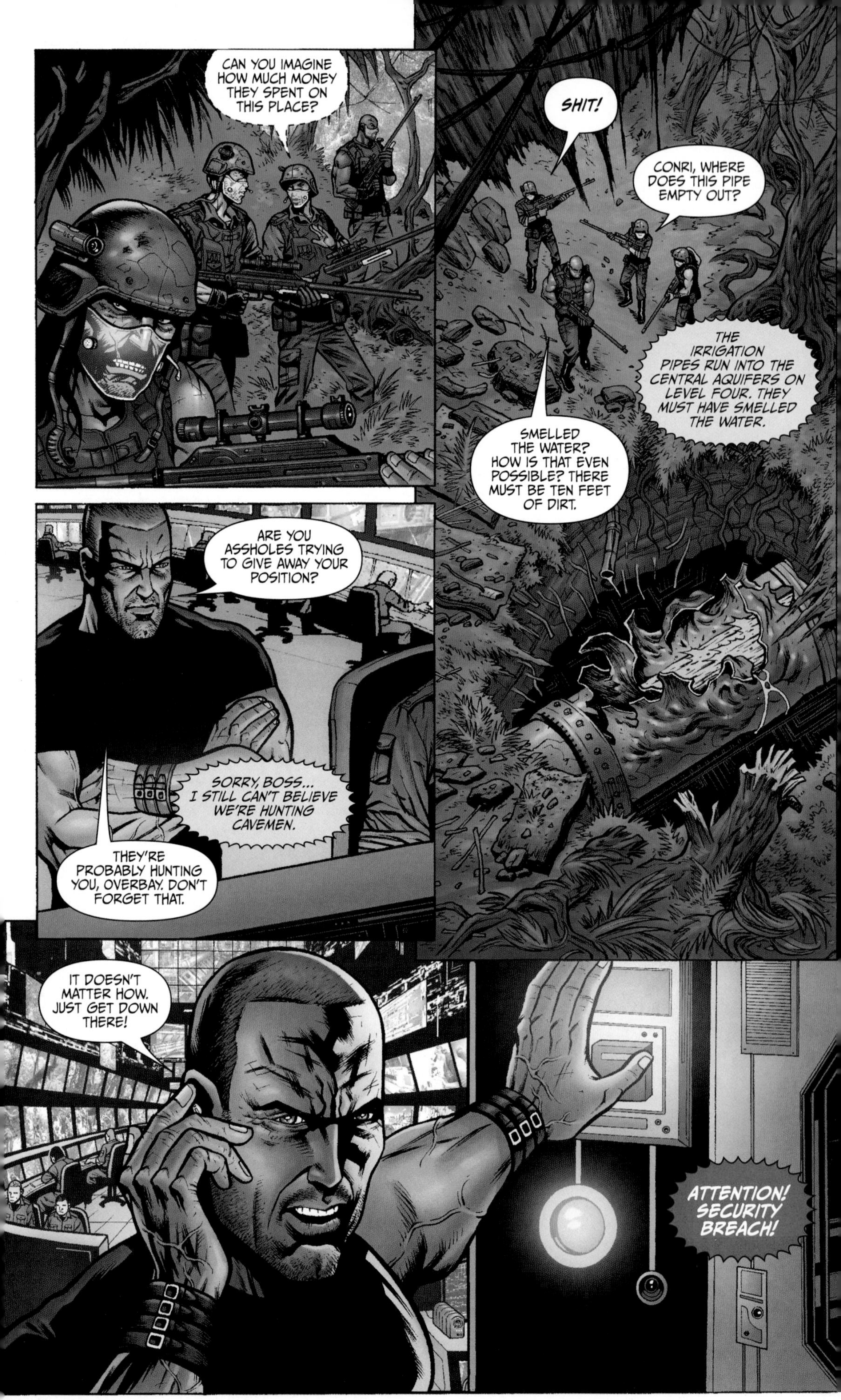
CAN YOU IMAGINE HOW MUCH MONEY THEY SPENT ON THIS PLACE?
SHIT!
CONRI, WHERE DOES THIS PIPE EMPTY OUT?
THE IRRIGATION PIPES RUN INTO THE CENTRAL AQUIFERS ON LEVEL FOUR. THEY MUST HAVE SMELLED THE WATER.
SMELLED THE WATER? HOW IS THAT EVEN POSSIBLE? THERE MUST BE TEN FEET OF DIRT.
ARE YOU ASSHOLES TRYING TO GIVE AWAY YOUR POSITION?
SORRY, BOSS... I STILL CAN'T BELIEVE WE'RE HUNTING CAVEMEN.
THEY'RE PROBABLY HUNTING YOU, OVERBAY. DON'T FORGET THAT.
IT DOESN'T MATTER HOW. JUST GET DOWN THERE!
ATTENTION! SECURITY BREACH!

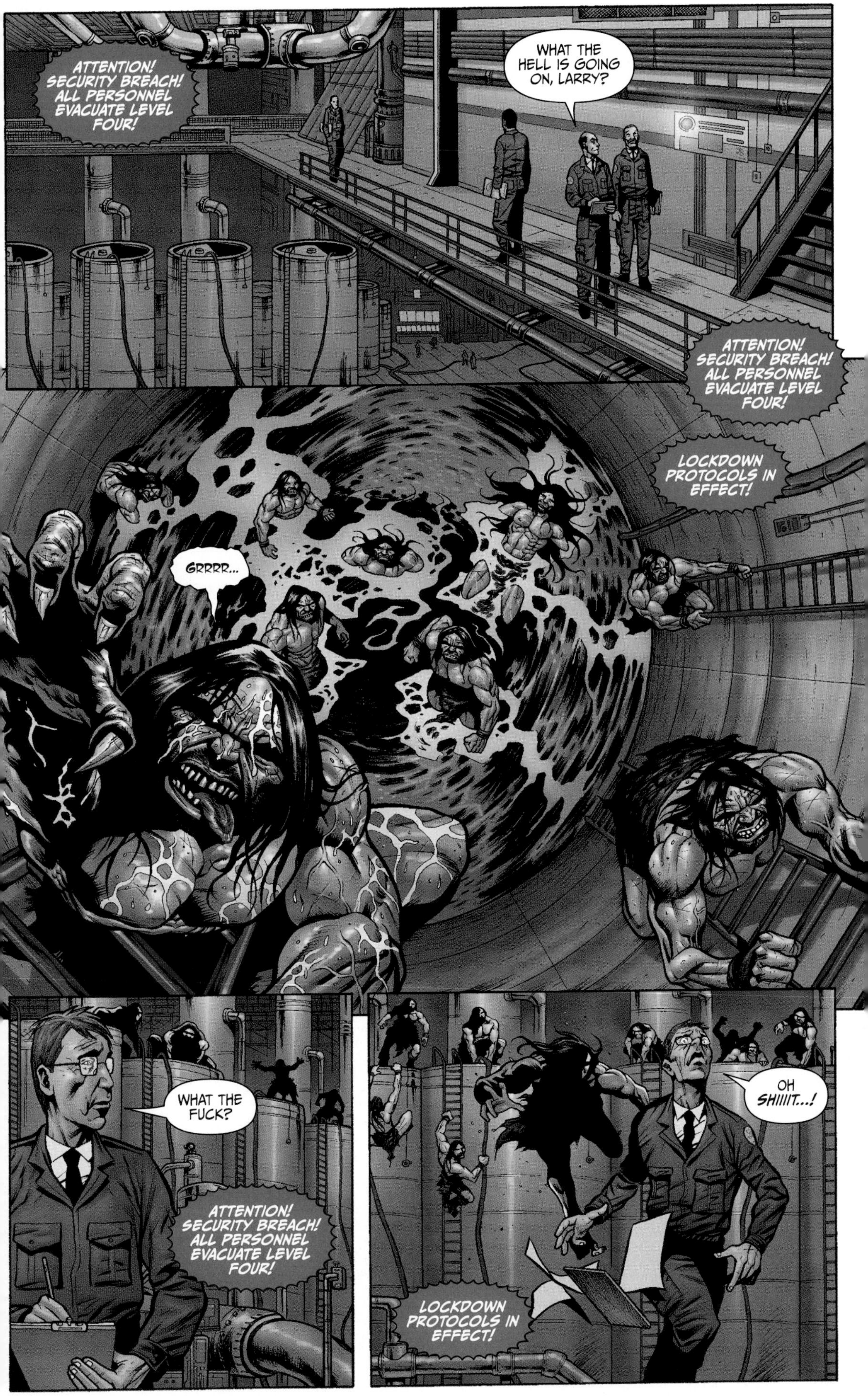

ATTENTION! SECURITY BREACH! ALL PERSONNEL EVACUATE LEVEL FOUR!
WHAT THE HELL IS GOING ON, LARRY?
ATTENTION! SECURITY BREACH! ALL PERSONNEL EVACUATE LEVEL FOUR!
LOCKDOWN PROTOCOLS IN EFFECT!
GRRRR...
WHAT THE FUCK?
ATTENTION! SECURITY BREACH! ALL PERSONNEL EVACUATE LEVEL FOUR!
OH SHIIIIT...!
LOCKDOWN PROTOCOLS IN EFFECT!

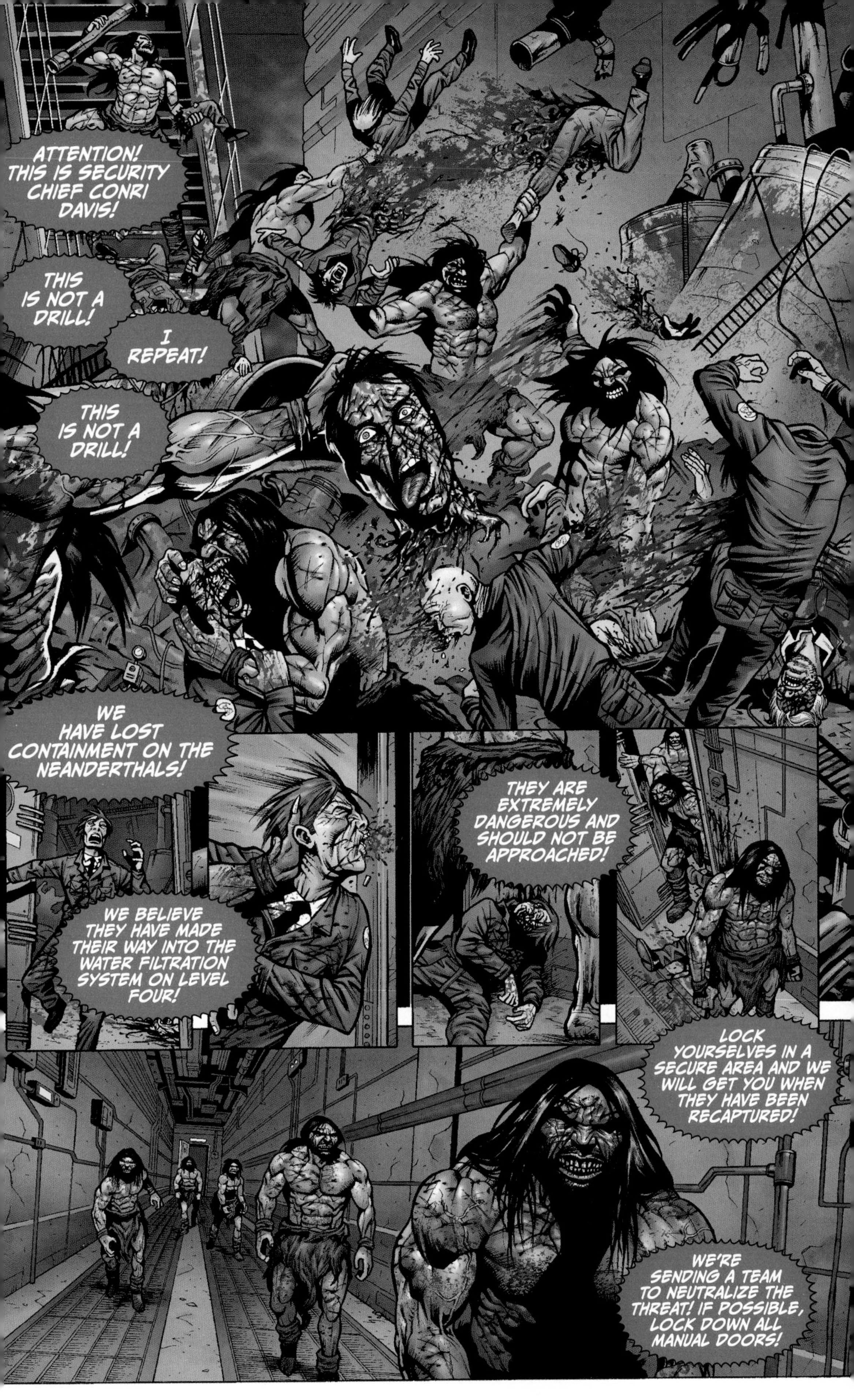
ATTENTION! THIS IS SECURITY CHIEF CONRI DAVIS!
THIS IS NOT A DRILL!
I REPEAT!
THIS IS NOT A DRILL!
WE HAVE LOST CONTAINMENT ON THE NEANDERTHALS!
WE BELIEVE THEY HAVE MADE THEIR WAY INTO THE WATER FILTRATION SYSTEM ON LEVEL FOUR!
THEY ARE EXTREMELY DANGEROUS AND SHOULD NOT BE APPROACHED!
LOCK YOURSELVES IN A SECURE AREA AND WE WILL GET YOU WHEN THEY HAVE BEEN RECAPTURED!
WE'RE SENDING A TEAM TO NEUTRALIZE THE THREAT! IF POSSIBLE, LOCK DOWN ALL MANUAL DOORS!

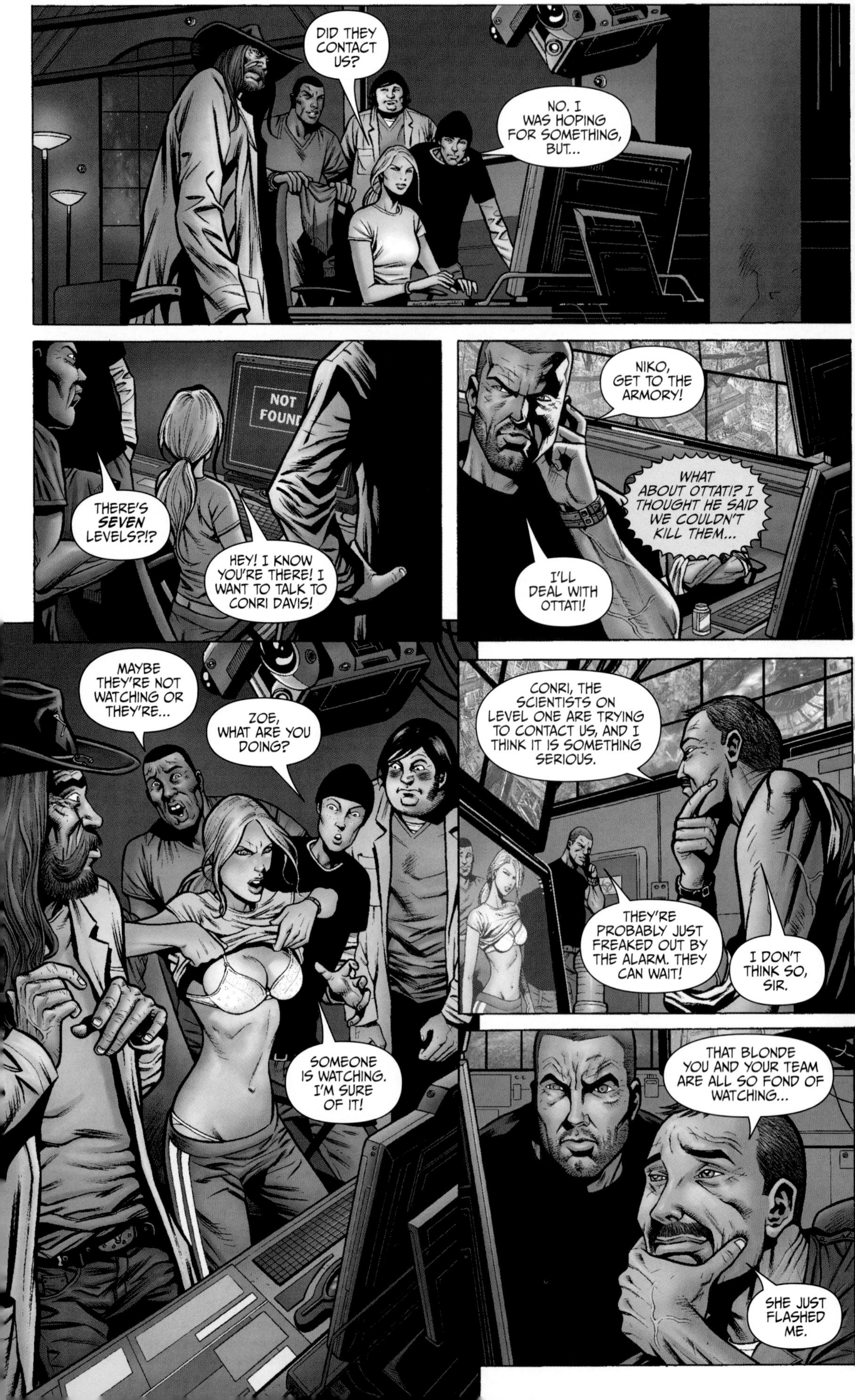
DID THEY CONTACT US?
NO. I WAS HOPING FOR SOMETHING, BUT...
THERE'S SEVEN LEVELS?!?
NOT FOUND
HEY! I KNOW YOU'RE THERE! I WANT TO TALK TO CONRI DAVIS!
NIKO, GET TO THE ARMORY!
WHAT ABOUT OTTATI!? I THOUGHT HE SAID WE COULDN'T KILL THEM...
I'LL DEAL WITH OTTATI!
MAYBE THEY'RE NOT WATCHING OR THEY'RE...
ZOE, WHAT ARE YOU DOING?
SOMEONE IS WATCHING. I'M SURE OF IT!
CONRI, THE SCIENTISTS ON LEVEL ONE ARE TRYING TO CONTACT US, AND I THINK IT IS SOMETHING SERIOUS.
THEY'RE PROBABLY JUST FREAKED OUT BY THE ALARM. THEY CAN WAIT!
I DON'T THINK SO, SIR.
THAT BLONDE YOU AND YOUR TEAM ARE ALL SO FOND OF WATCHING...
SHE JUST FLASHED ME.

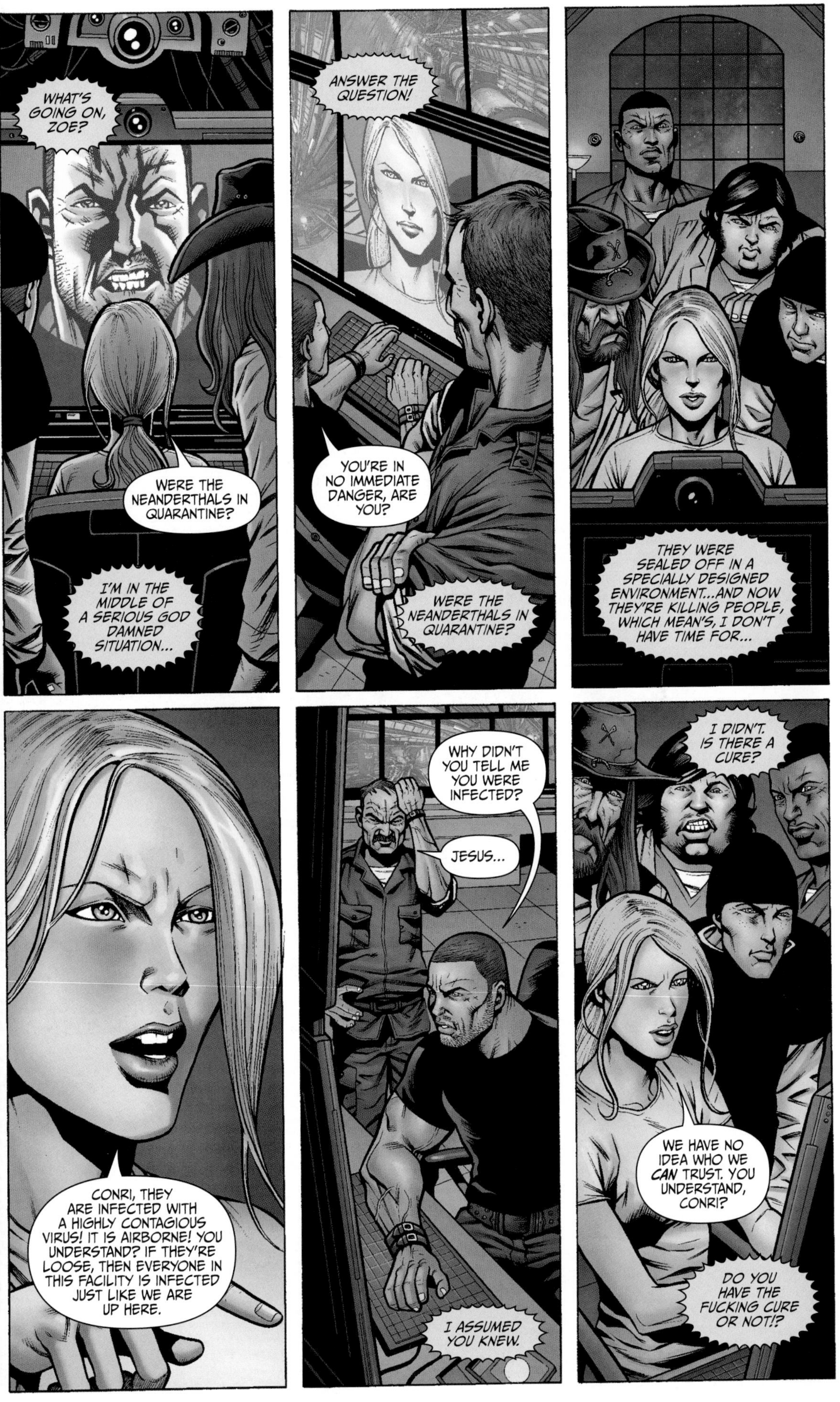
WHAT'S GOING ON, ZOE?
WERE THE NEANDERTHALS IN QUARANTINE?
I'M IN THE MIDDLE OF A SERIOUS GOD DAMNED SITUATION...
ANSWER THE QUESTION!
YOU'RE IN NO IMMEDIATE DANGER, ARE YOU?
WERE THE NEANDERTHALS IN QUARANTINE?
THEY WERE SEALED OFF IN A SPECIALLY DESIGNED ENVIRONMENT...AND NOW THEY'RE KILLING PEOPLE, WHICH MEAN'S, I DON'T HAVE TIME FOR...
CONRI, THEY ARE INFECTED WITH A HIGHLY CONTAGIOUS VIRUS! IT IS AIRBORNE! YOU UNDERSTAND? IF THEY'RE LOOSE, THEN EVERYONE IN THIS FACILITY IS INFECTED JUST LIKE WE ARE UP HERE.
WHY DIDN'T YOU TELL ME YOU WERE INFECTED?
JESUS...
I ASSUMED YOU KNEW.
I DIDN'T. IS THERE A CURE?
WE HAVE NO IDEA WHO WE CAN TRUST. YOU UNDERSTAND, CONRI?
DO YOU HAVE THE FUCKING CURE OR NOT!?

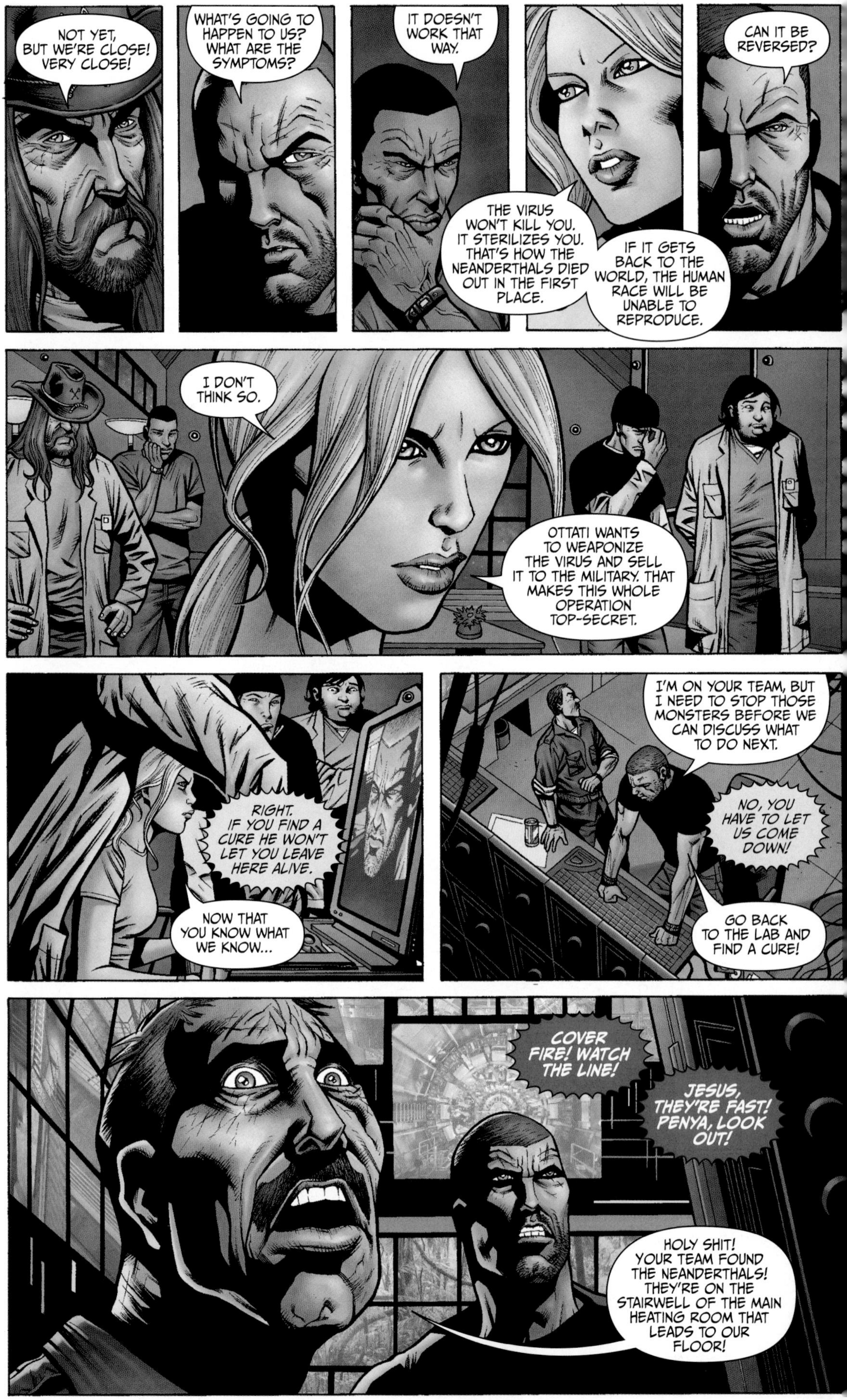
NOT YET, BUT WE'RE CLOSE! VERY CLOSE!
WHAT'S GOING TO HAPPEN TO US? WHAT ARE THE SYMPTOMS?
IT DOESN'T WORK THAT WAY.
THE VIRUS WON'T KILL YOU. IT STERILIZES YOU. THAT'S HOW THE NEANDERTHALS DIED OUT IN THE FIRST PLACE.
IF IT GETS BACK TO THE WORLD, THE HUMAN RACE WILL BE UNABLE TO REPRODUCE.
CAN IT BE REVERSED?
I DON'T THINK SO.
OTTATI WANTS TO WEAPONIZE THE VIRUS AND SELL IT TO THE MILITARY. THAT MAKES THIS WHOLE OPERATION TOP-SECRET.
RIGHT. IF YOU FIND A CURE HE WON'T LET YOU LEAVE HERE ALIVE.
NOW THAT YOU KNOW WHAT WE KNOW...
I'M ON YOUR TEAM, BUT I NEED TO STOP THOSE MONSTERS BEFORE WE CAN DISCUSS WHAT TO DO NEXT.
NO, YOU HAVE TO LET US COME DOWN!
GO BACK TO THE LAB AND FIND A CURE!
COVER FIRE! WATCH THE LINE!
JESUS, THEY'RE FAST! PENYA, LOOK OUT!
HOLY SHIT! YOUR TEAM FOUND THE NEANDERTHALS! THEY'RE ON THE STAIRWELL OF THE MAIN HEATING ROOM THAT LEADS TO OUR FLOOR!

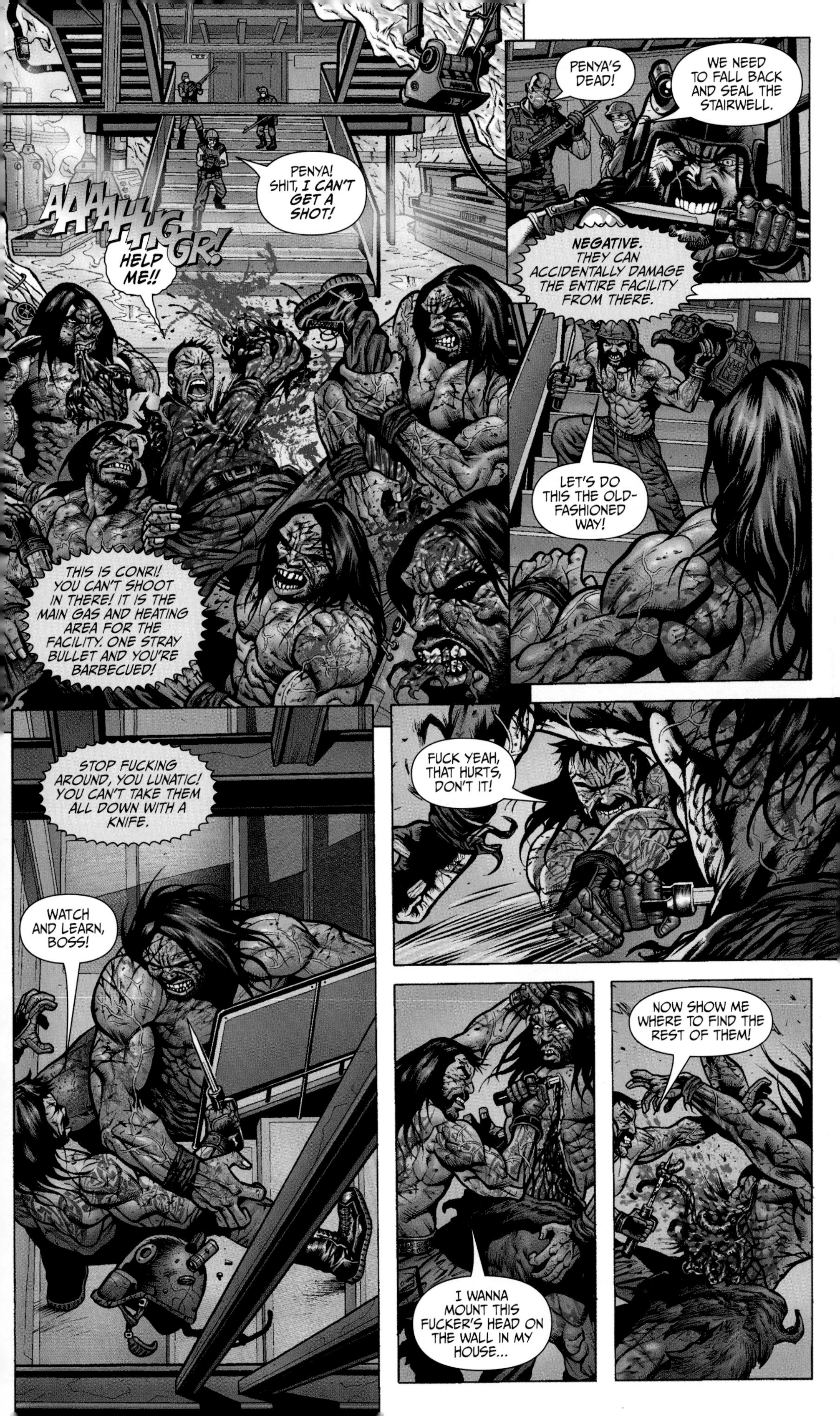
PENYA! SHIT, I CAN'T GET A SHOT!
AAAAHHGGR!
HELP ME!!
THIS IS CONRI! YOU CAN'T SHOOT IN THERE! IT IS THE MAIN GAS AND HEATING AREA FOR THE FACILITY. ONE STRAY BULLET AND YOU'RE BARBECUED!
PENYA'S DEAD!
WE NEED TO FALL BACK AND SEAL THE STAIRWELL.
NEGATIVE. THEY CAN ACCIDENTALLY DAMAGE THE ENTIRE FACILITY FROM THERE.
LET'S DO THIS THE OLD-FASHIONED WAY!
STOP FUCKING AROUND, YOU LUNATIC! YOU CAN'T TAKE THEM ALL DOWN WITH A KNIFE.
WATCH AND LEARN, BOSS!
FUCK YEAH, THAT HURTS, DON'T IT!
I WANNA MOUNT THIS FUCKER'S HEAD ON THE WALL IN MY HOUSE...
NOW SHOW ME WHERE TO FIND THE REST OF THEM!

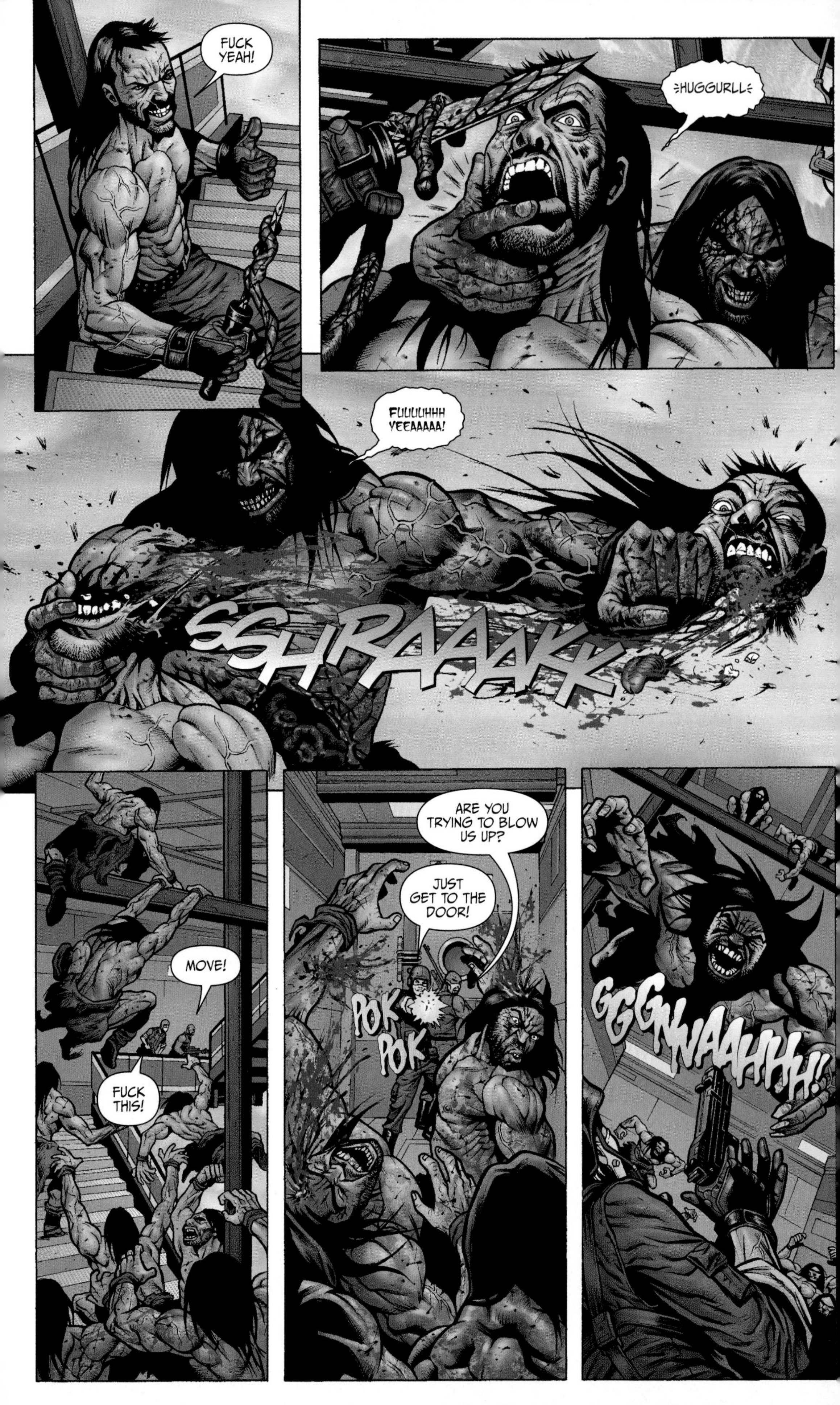
FUCK YEAH!
HUGGURLL
FUUUUHHH YEEAAAAA!
SSHRAAAKK
MOVE!
FUCK THIS!
ARE YOU TRYING TO BLOW US UP?
JUST GET TO THE DOOR!
POK
POK
GGGNAAHHH!

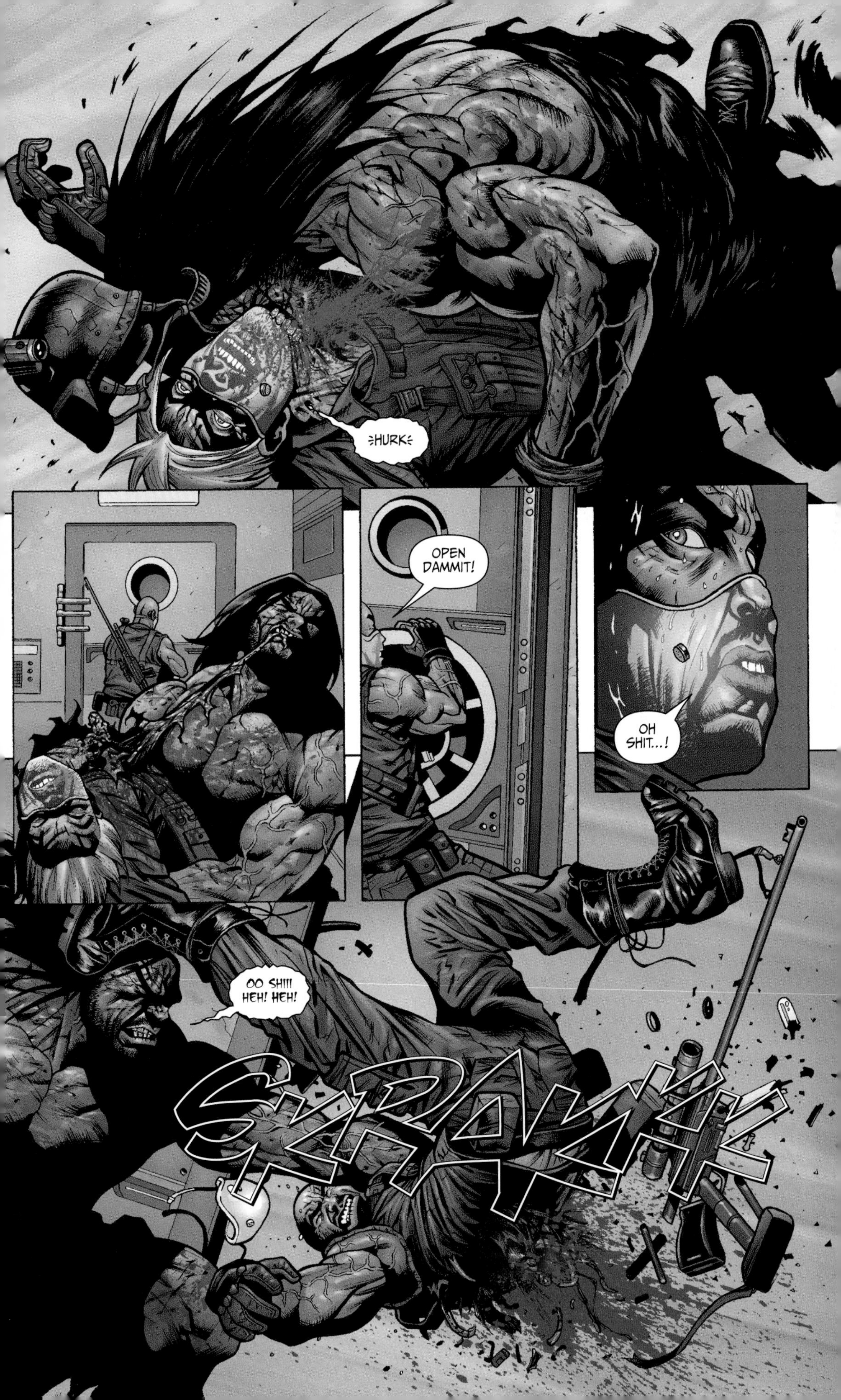

HURK
OPEN DAMMIT!
OH SHIT...!
OO SHIII HEH! HEH!
SKRAKK

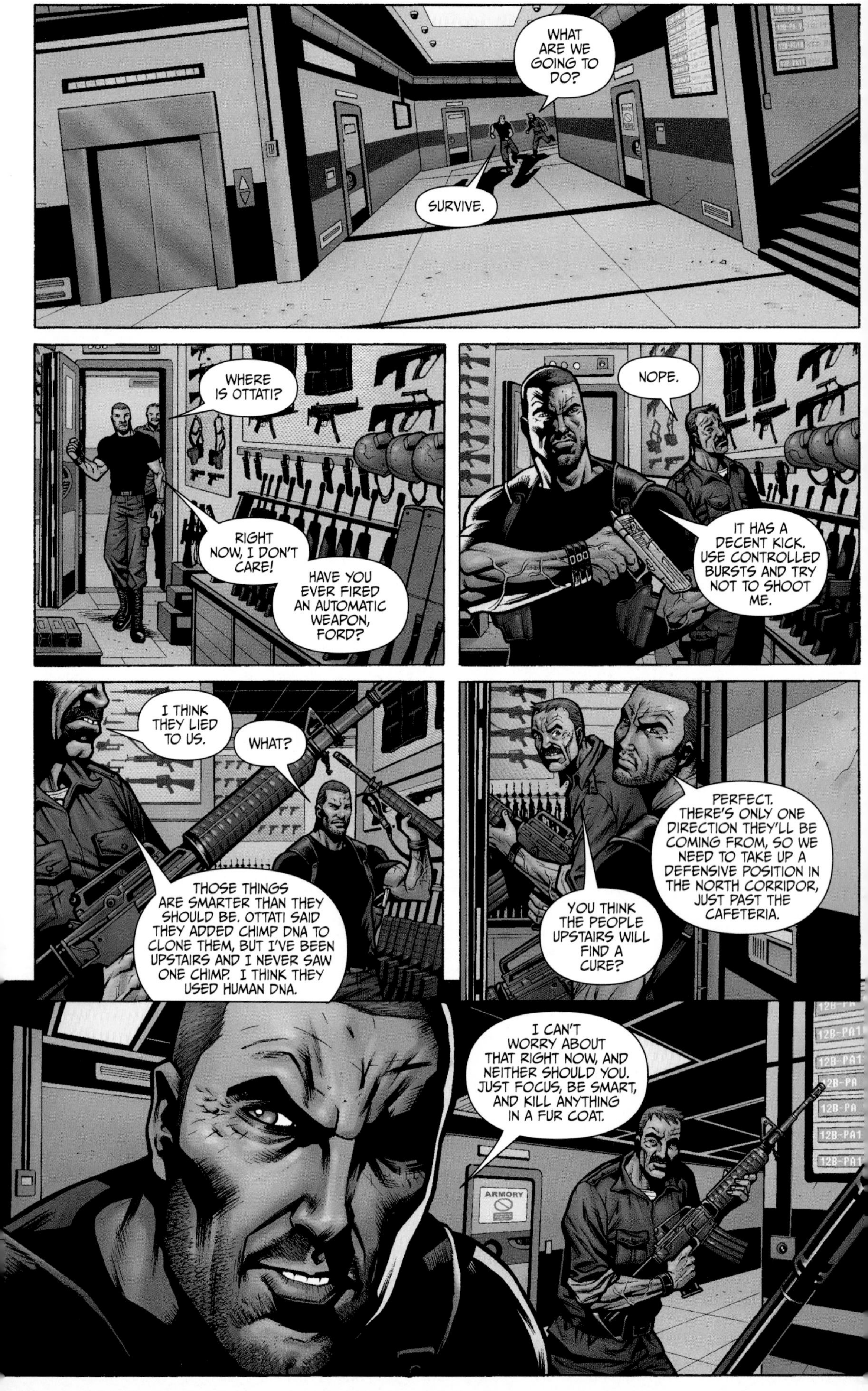

WHAT ARE WE GOING TO DO?
SURVIVE.
WHERE IS OTTATI?
RIGHT NOW, I DON'T CARE!
HAVE YOU EVER FIRED AN AUTOMATIC WEAPON, FORD?
NOPE.
IT HAS A DECENT KICK. USE CONTROLLED BURSTS AND TRY NOT TO SHOOT ME.
I THINK THEY LIED TO US.
WHAT?
THOSE THINGS ARE SMARTER THAN THEY SHOULD BE. OTTATI SAID THEY ADDED CHIMP DNA TO CLONE THEM, BUT I'VE BEEN UPSTAIRS AND I NEVER SAW ONE CHIMP. I THINK THEY USED HUMAN DNA.
PERFECT. THERE'S ONLY ONE DIRECTION THEY'LL BE COMING FROM, SO WE NEED TO TAKE UP A DEFENSIVE POSITION IN THE NORTH CORRIDOR, JUST PAST THE CAFETERIA.
YOU THINK THE PEOPLE UPSTAIRS WILL FIND A CURE?
I CAN'T WORRY ABOUT THAT RIGHT NOW, AND NEITHER SHOULD YOU. JUST FOCUS, BE SMART, AND KILL ANYTHING IN A FUR COAT.
ARMORY

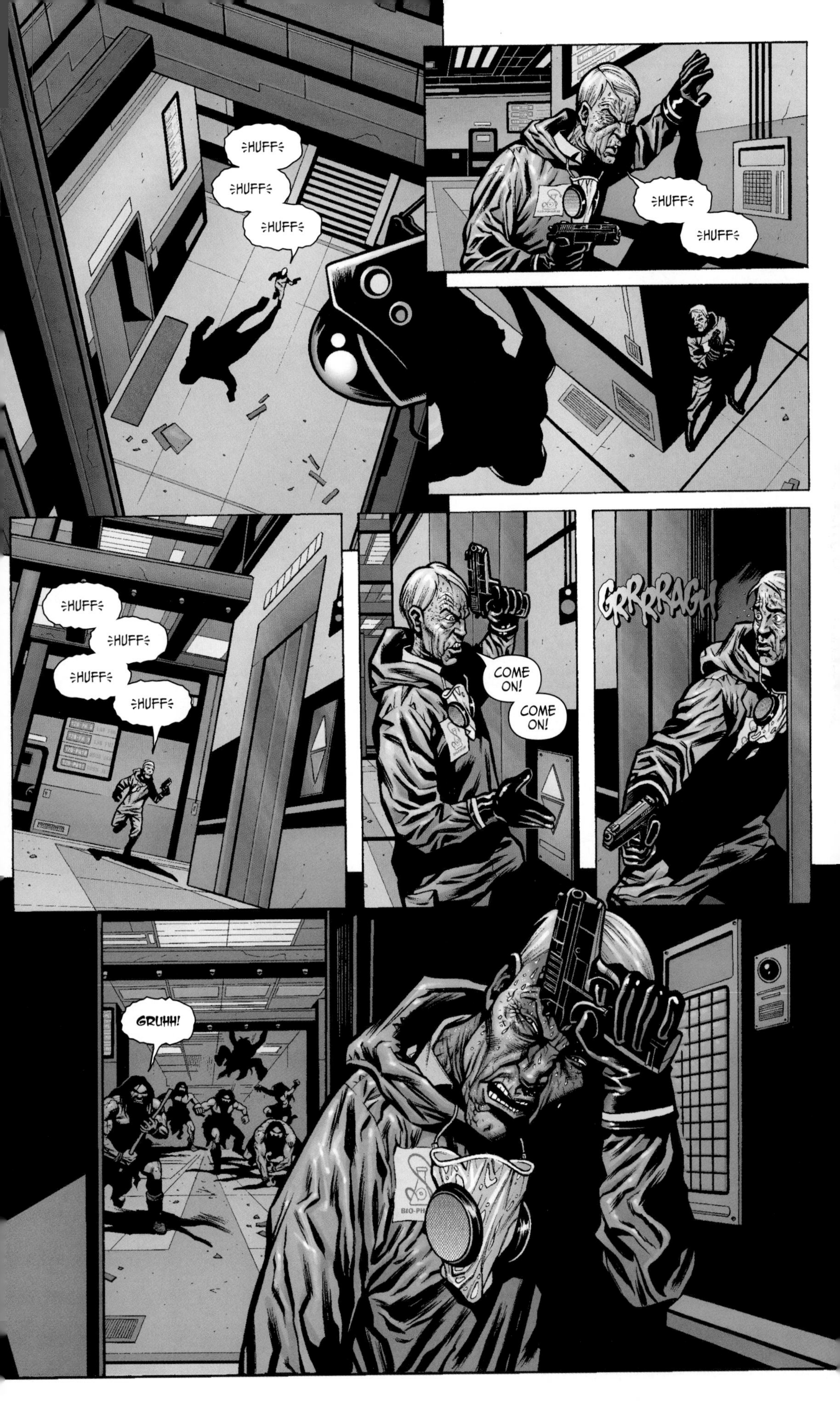

HUFF
HUFF
HUFF
HUFF
HUFF
HUFF
HUFF
HUFF
HUFF
COME ON!
COME ON!
GRRRRAGH
GRUHH!

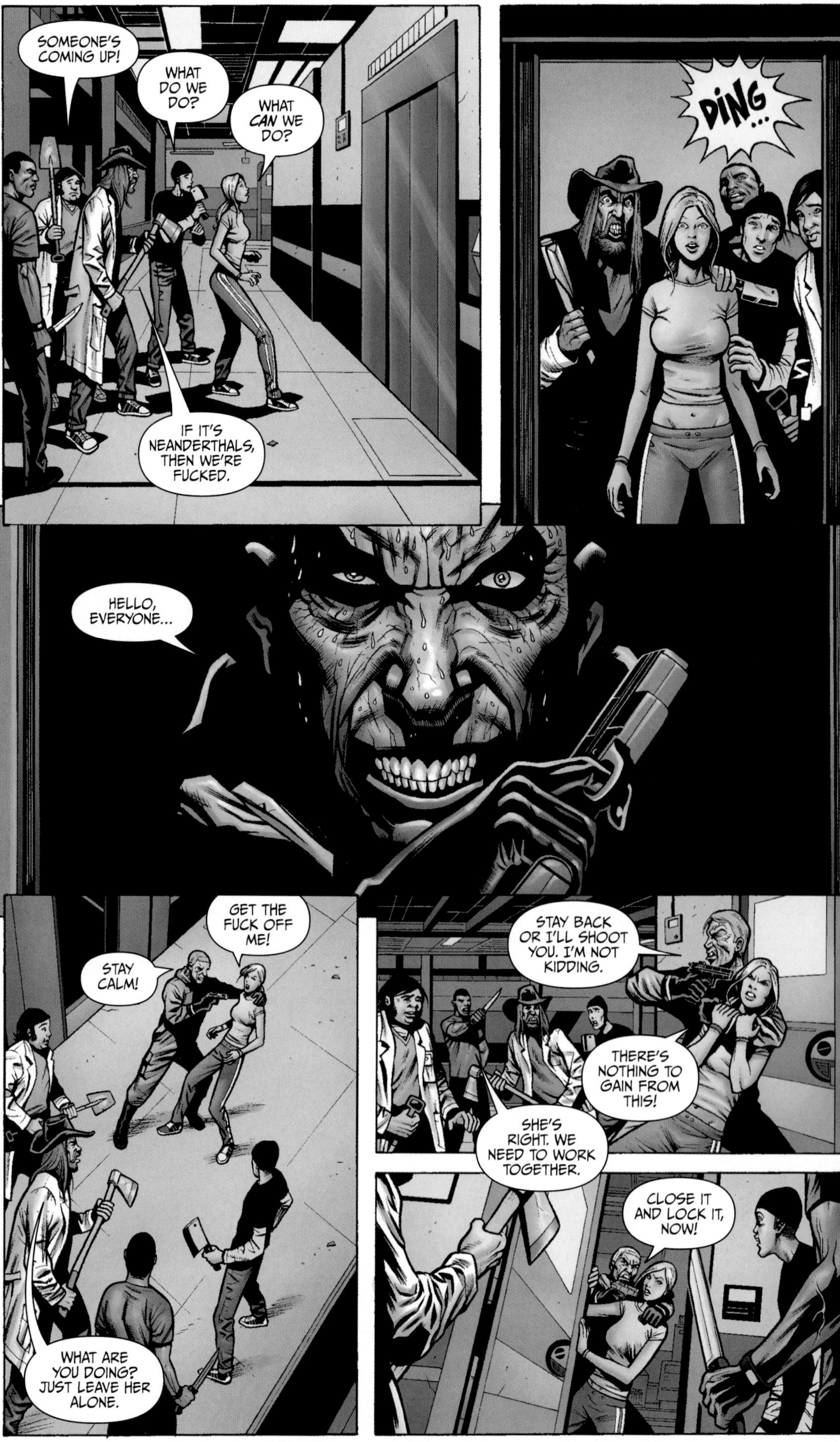
SOMEONE'S COMING UP!
WHAT DO WE DO?
WHAT CAN WE DO?
IF IT'S NEANDERTHALS, THEN WE'RE FUCKED.
DING...
HELLO, EVERYONE...
GET THE FUCK OFF ME!
STAY CALM!
WHAT ARE YOU DOING? JUST LEAVE HER ALONE.
STAY BACK OR I'LL SHOOT YOU. I'M NOT KIDDING.
THERE'S NOTHING TO GAIN FROM THIS!
SHE'S RIGHT. WE NEED TO WORK TOGETHER.
CLOSE IT AND LOCK IT, NOW!

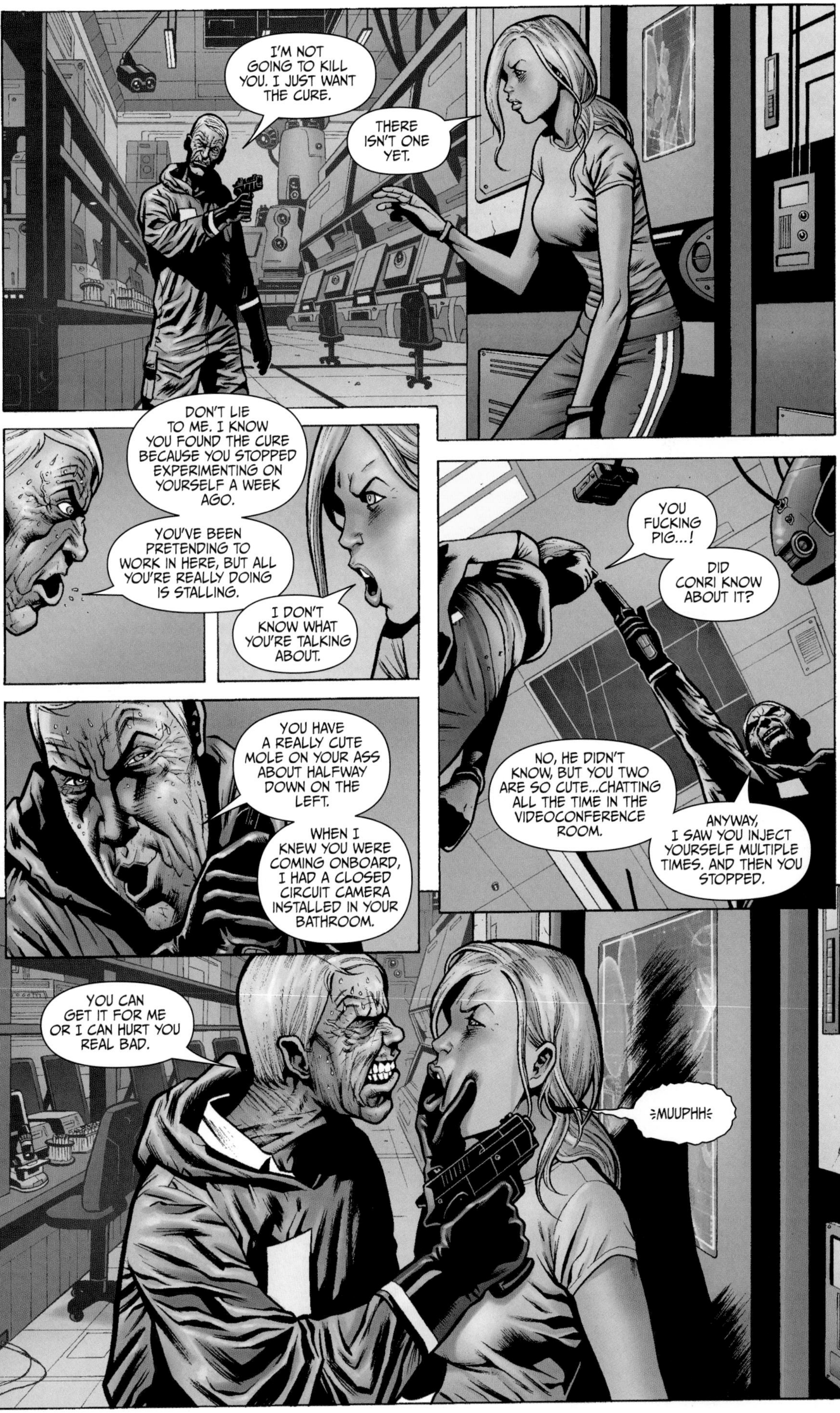
I'M NOT GOING TO KILL YOU. I JUST WANT THE CURE.
THERE ISN'T ONE YET.
DON'T LIE TO ME. I KNOW YOU FOUND THE CURE BECAUSE YOU STOPPED EXPERIMENTING ON YOURSELF A WEEK AGO.
YOU'VE BEEN PRETENDING TO WORK IN HERE, BUT ALL YOU'RE REALLY DOING IS STALLING.
I DON'T KNOW WHAT YOU'RE TALKING ABOUT.
YOU FUCKING PIG...!
DID CONRI KNOW ABOUT IT?
NO, HE DIDN'T KNOW, BUT YOU TWO ARE SO CUTE...CHATTING ALL THE TIME IN THE VIDEOCONFERENCE ROOM.
ANYWAY, I SAW YOU INJECT YOURSELF MULTIPLE TIMES. AND THEN YOU STOPPED.
YOU HAVE A REALLY CUTE MOLE ON YOUR ASS ABOUT HALFWAY DOWN ON THE LEFT.
WHEN I KNEW YOU WERE COMING ONBOARD, I HAD A CLOSED CIRCUIT CAMERA INSTALLED IN YOUR BATHROOM.
YOU CAN GET IT FOR ME OR I CAN HURT YOU REAL BAD.
MUUPHH

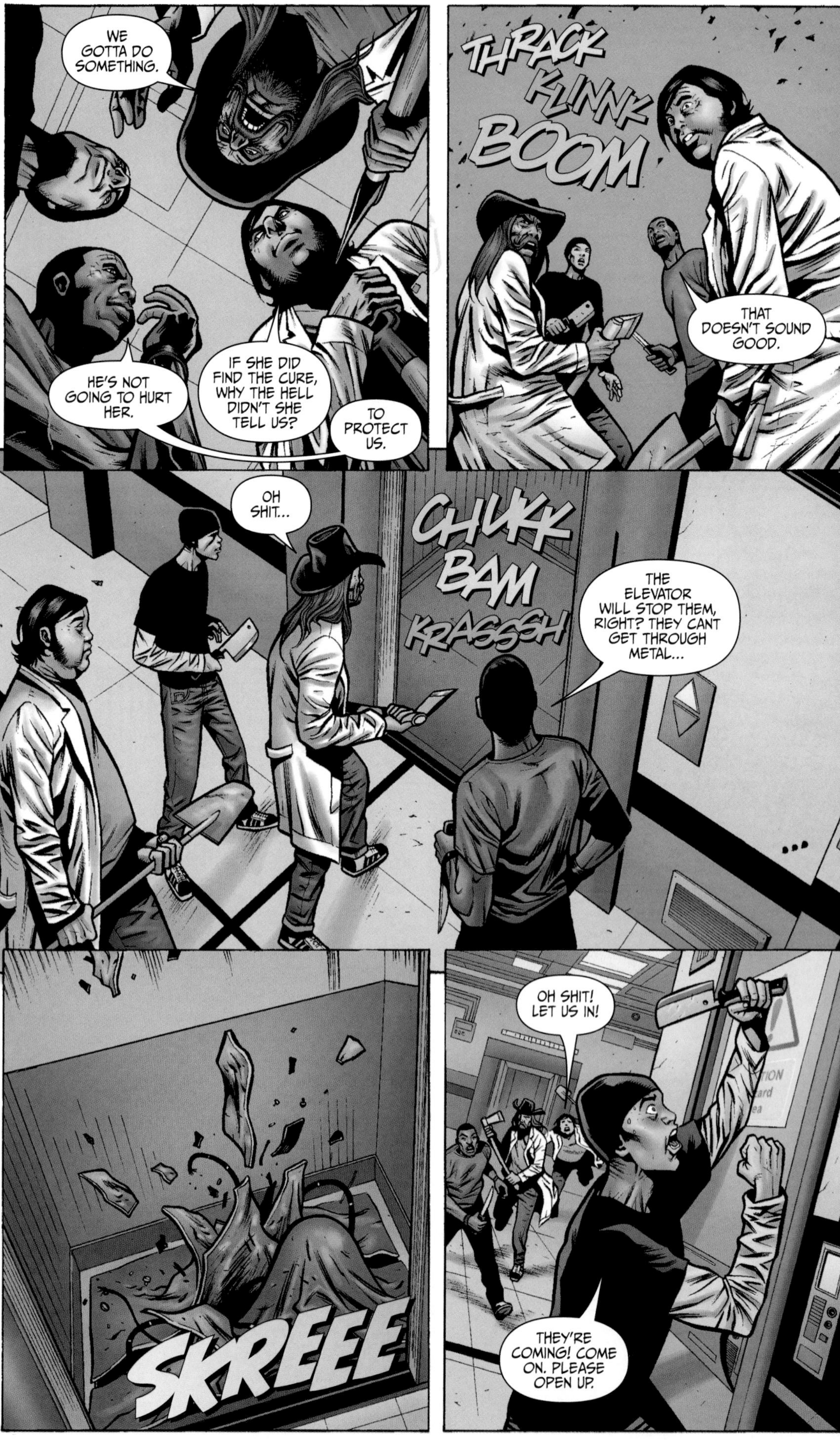
WE GOTTA DO SOMETHING.
HE'S NOT GOING TO HURT HER.
IF SHE DID FIND THE CURE, WHY THE HELL DIDN'T SHE TELL US?
TO PROTECT US.
THRACK
KLINNK
BOOM
THAT DOESN'T SOUND GOOD.
OH SHIT...
CHUKK
BAM
KRASSSH
THE ELEVATOR WILL STOP THEM, RIGHT? THEY CAN'T GET THROUGH METAL...
SKREEE
OH SHIT! LET US IN!
THEY'RE COMING! COME ON. PLEASE OPEN UP.

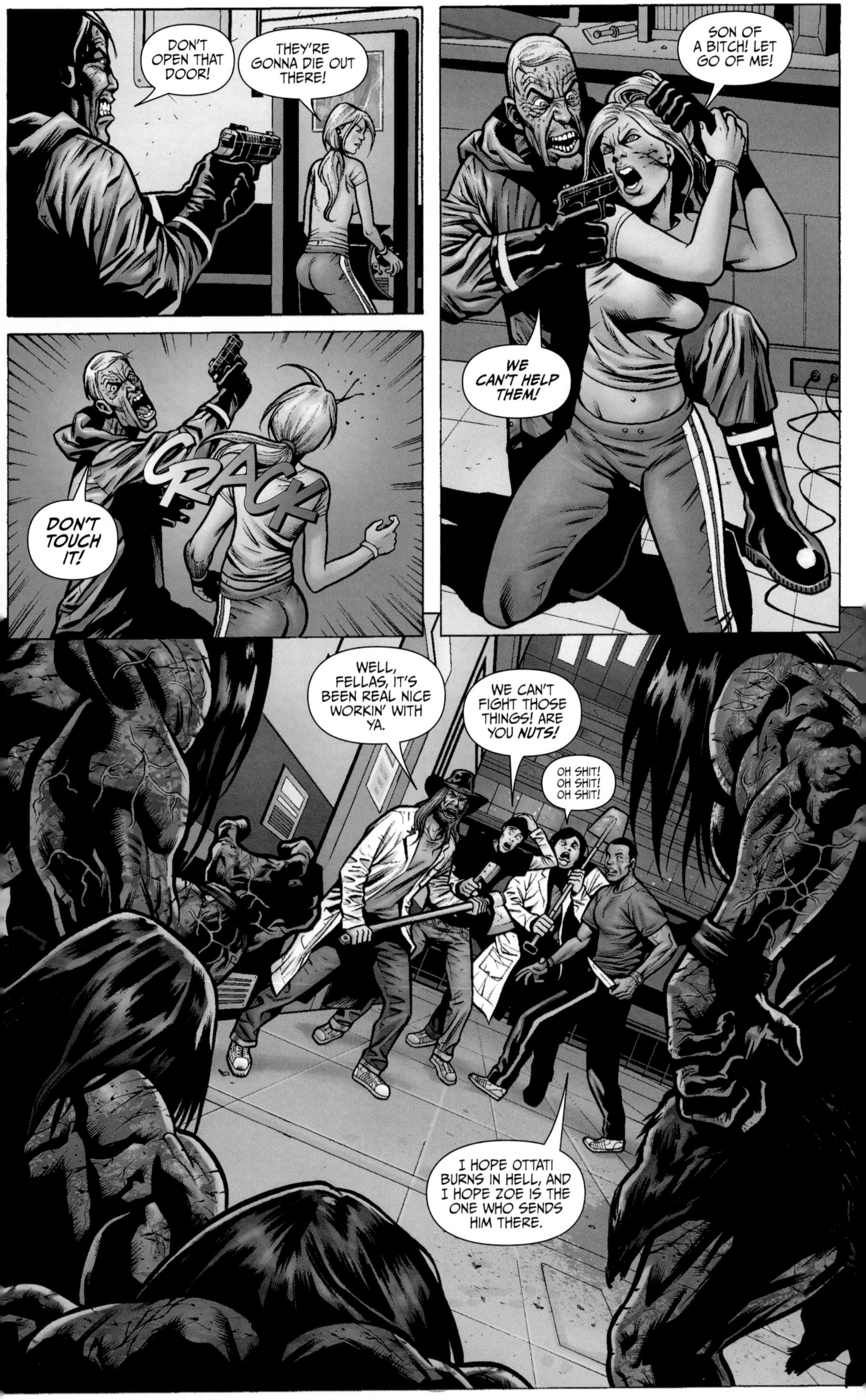
DON'T OPEN THAT DOOR!
THEY'RE GONNA DIE OUT THERE!
SON OF A BITCH! LET GO OF ME!
WE CAN'T HELP THEM!
CRACK
DON'T TOUCH IT!
WELL, FELLAS, IT'S BEEN REAL NICE WORKIN' WITH YA.
WE CAN'T FIGHT THOSE THINGS! ARE YOU NUTS!
OH SHIT! OH SHIT! OH SHIT!
I HOPE OTTATI BURNS IN HELL, AND I HOPE ZOE IS THE ONE WHO SENDS HIM THERE.

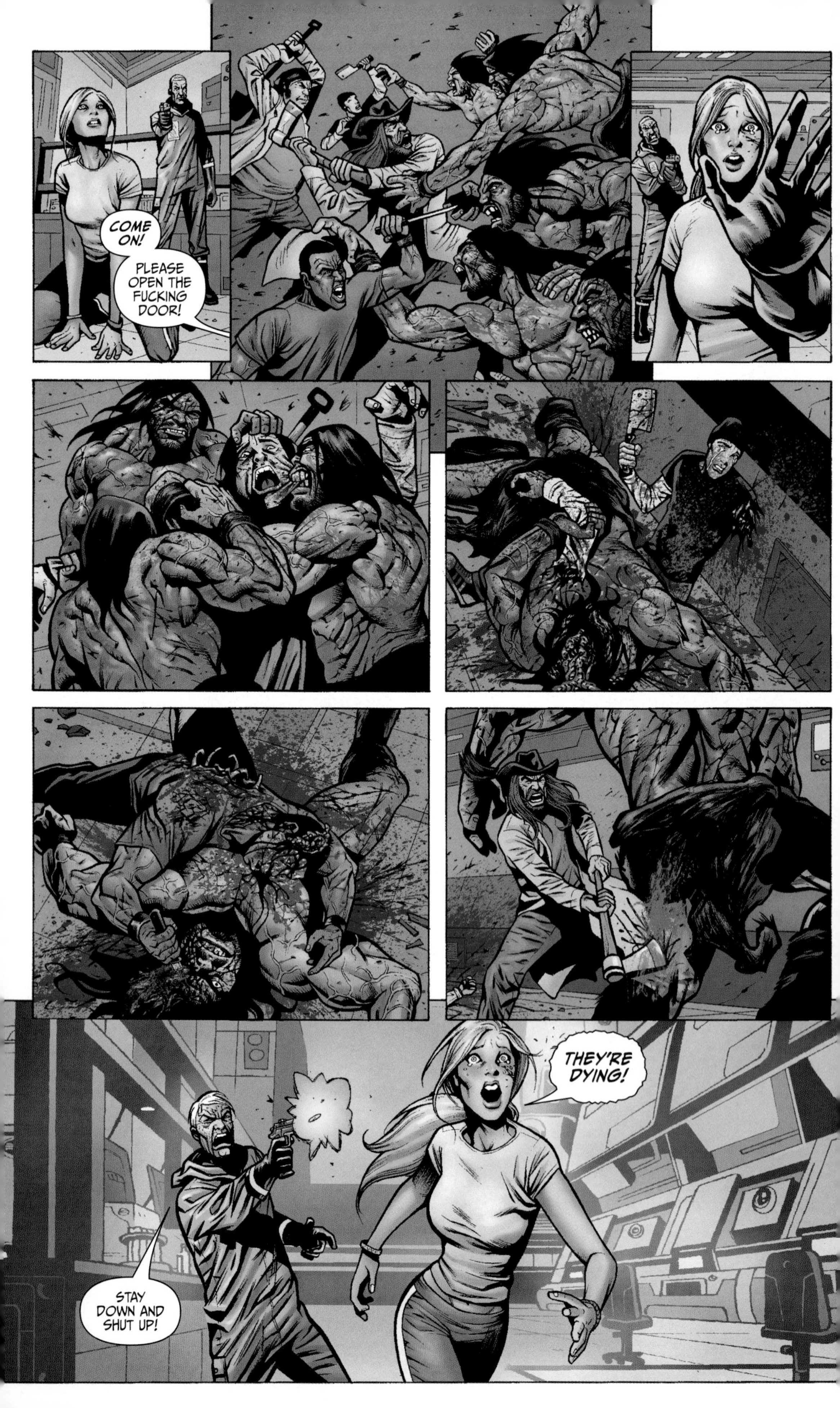
COME ON!
PLEASE OPEN THE FUCKING DOOR!
THEY'RE DYING!
STAY DOWN AND SHUT UP!

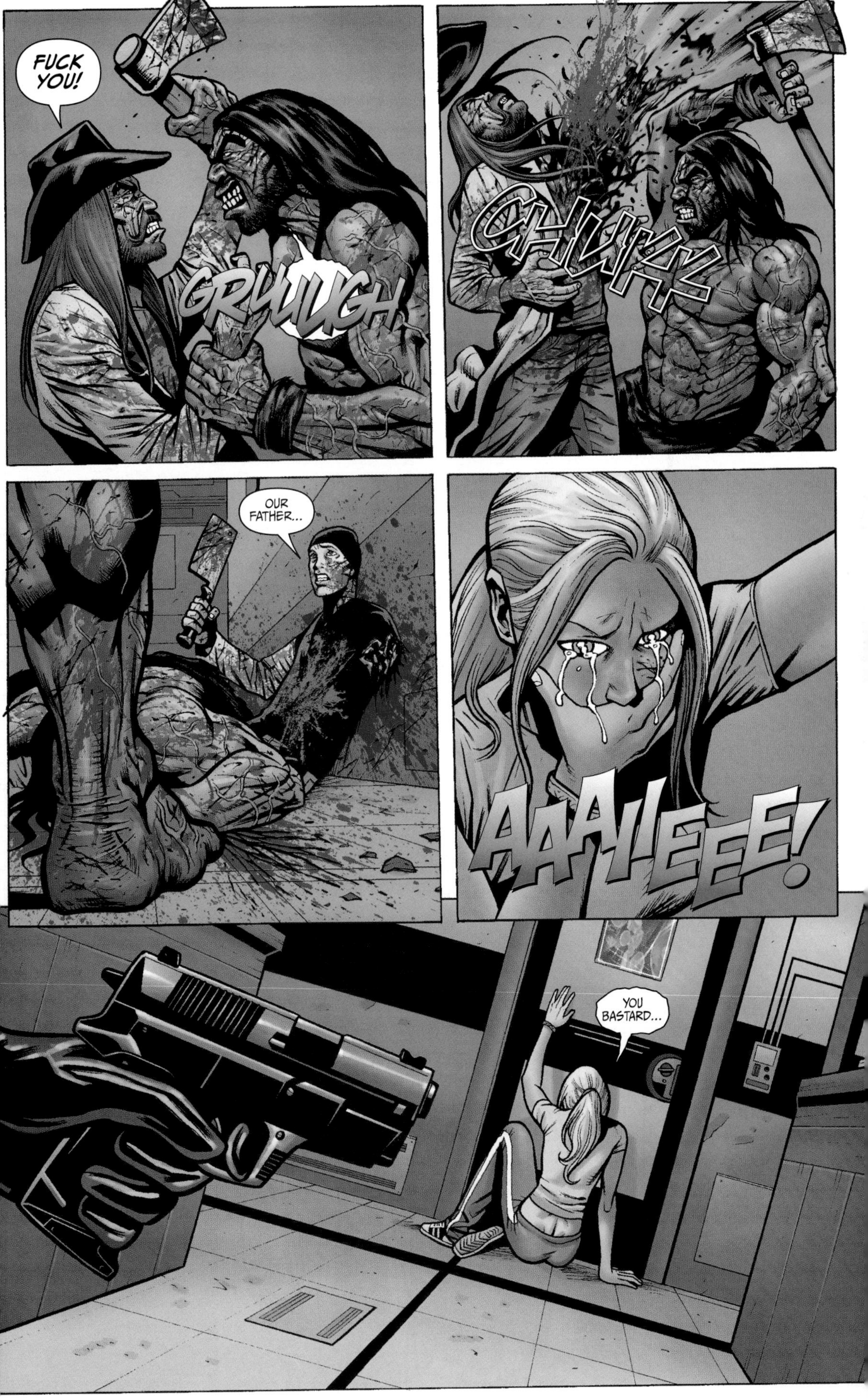

FUCK YOU!
GRUUUGH
CHUKK
OUR FATHER...
AAAIIEEEE!
YOU BASTARD...

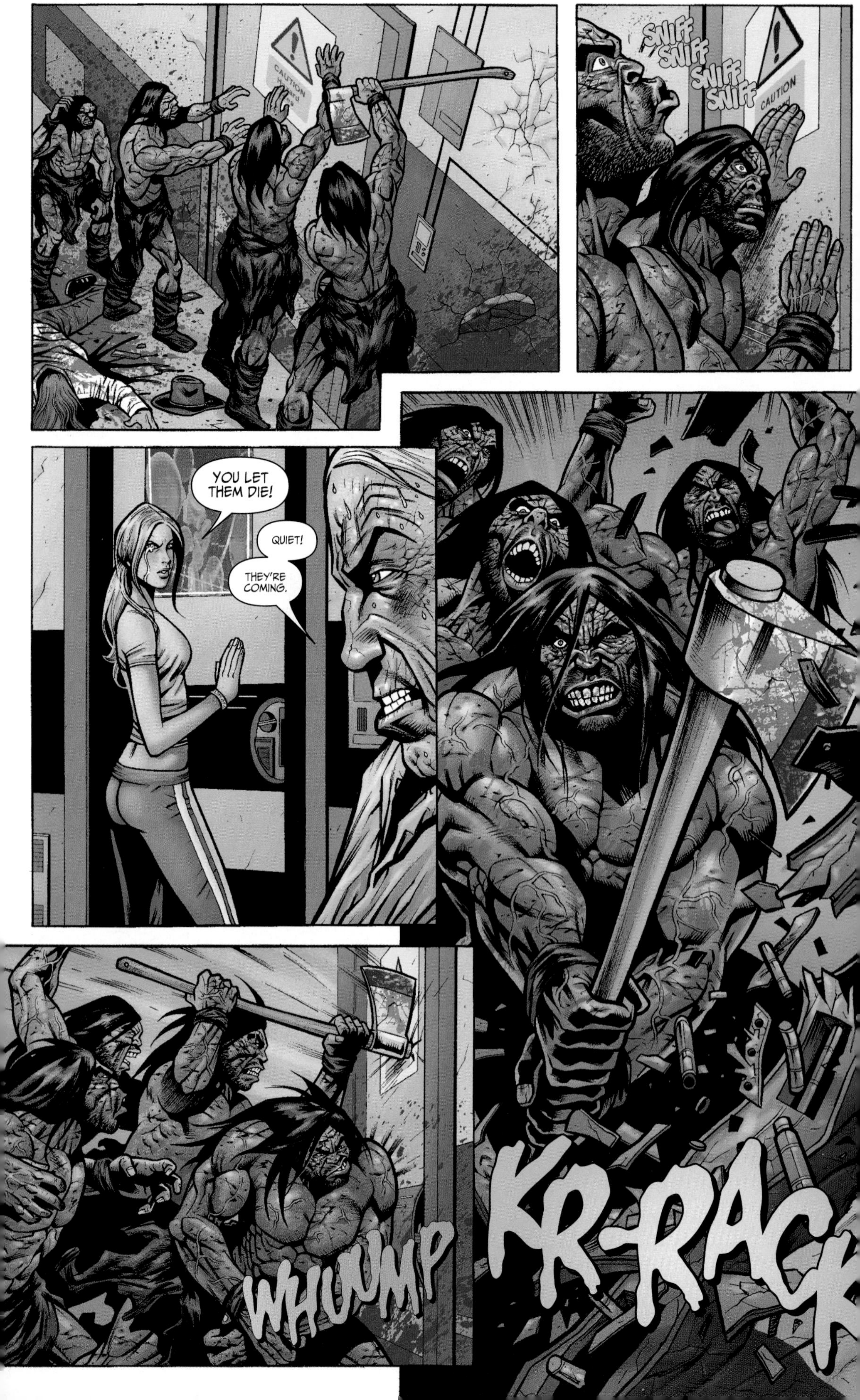

CAUTION
SNIFF SNIFF SNIFF SNIFF
CAUTION
YOU LET THEM DIE!
QUIET!
THEY'RE COMING.
WHUUMP
KR-RACK

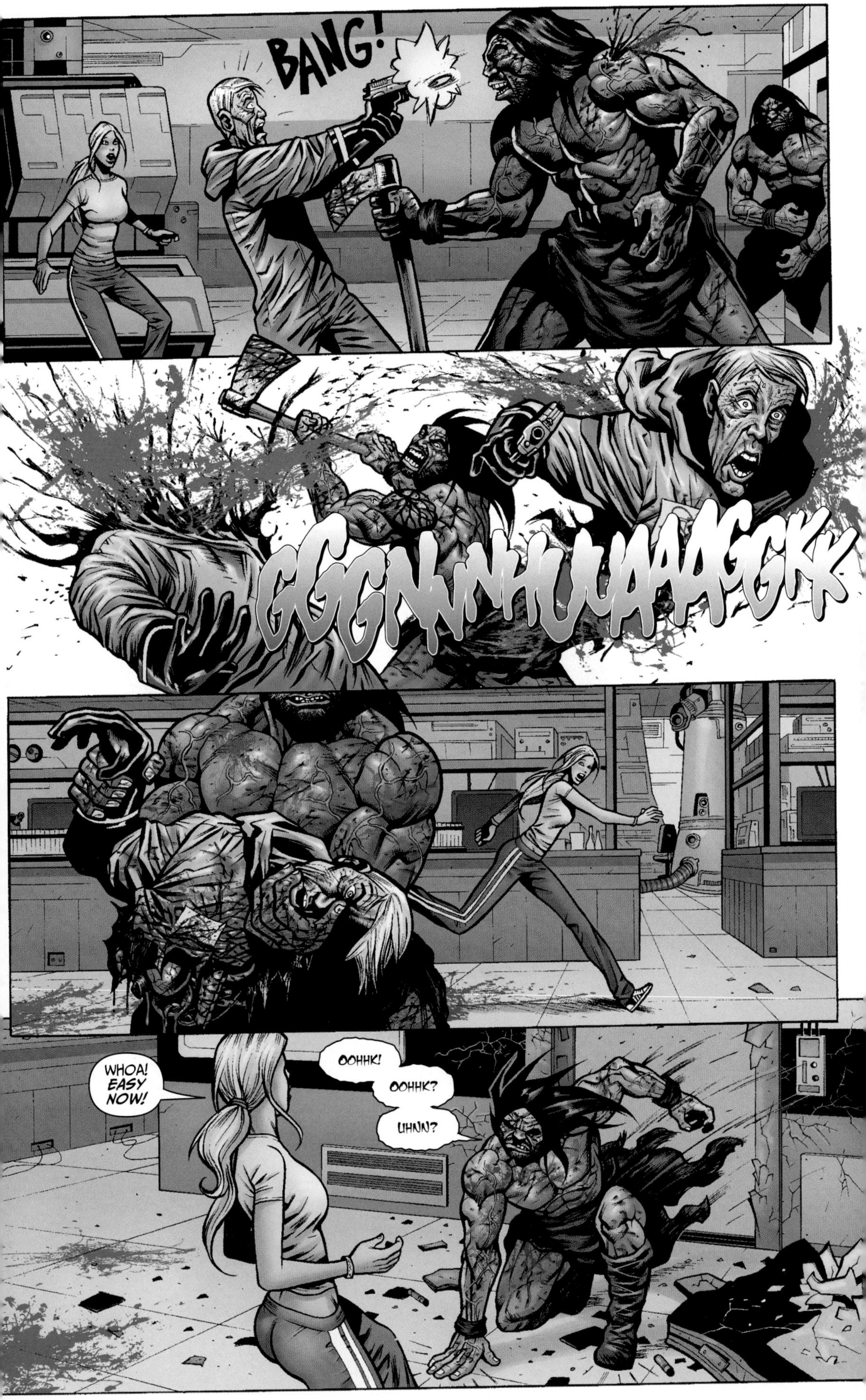
BANG!
GGGNNNHUUAAAGKK
WHOA! EASY NOW!
OOHHK!
OOHHK?
UHNN?

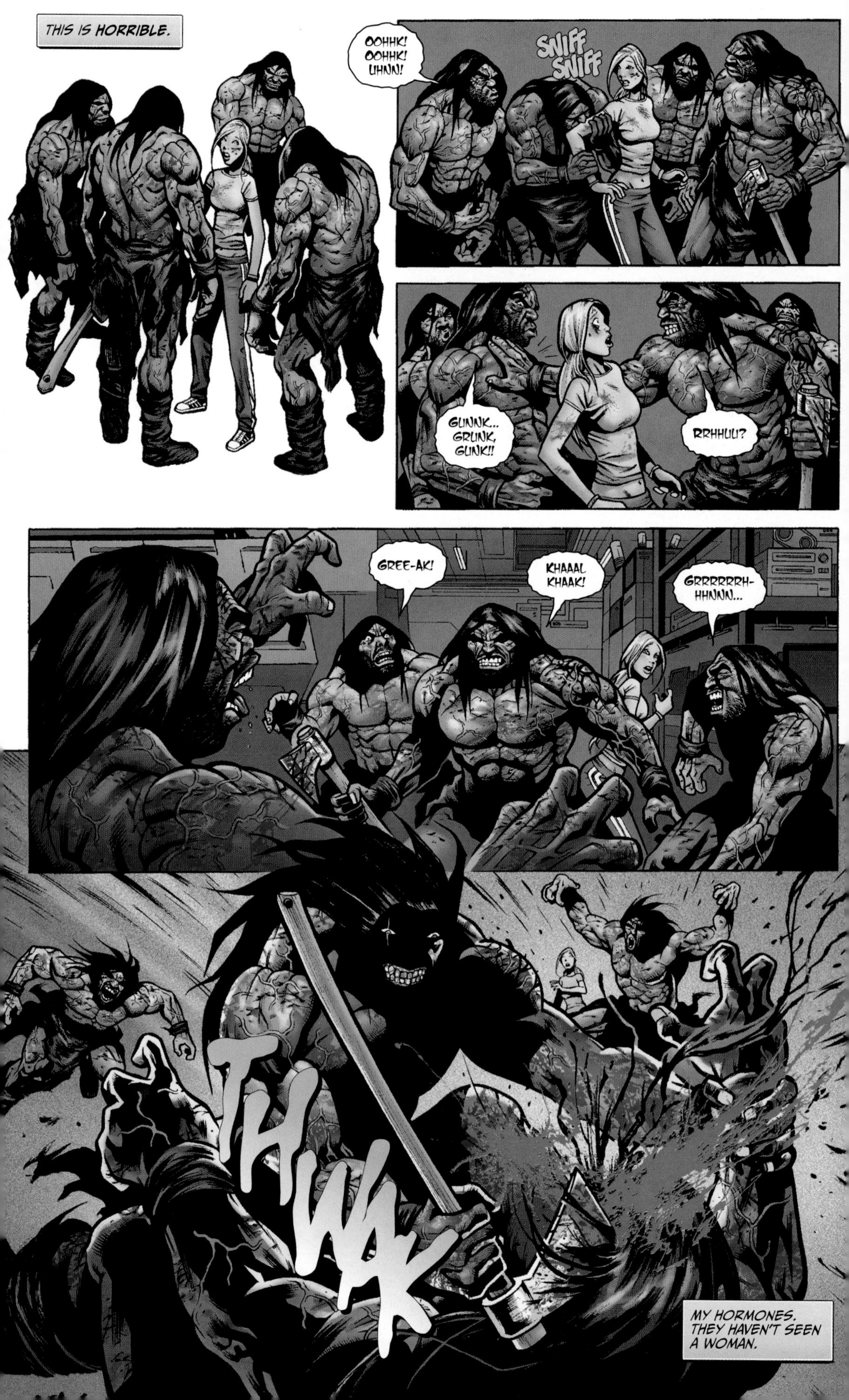
THIS IS HORRIBLE.
OOHHK! OOHHK! UHNN!
SNIFF SNIFF
GUNNK... GRUNK, GUNK!!
RRHHUU?
GREE-AK!
KHAAAL KHAAK!
GRRRRRRH-HHNNN...
THWAK
MY HORMONES. THEY HAVEN'T SEEN A WOMAN.

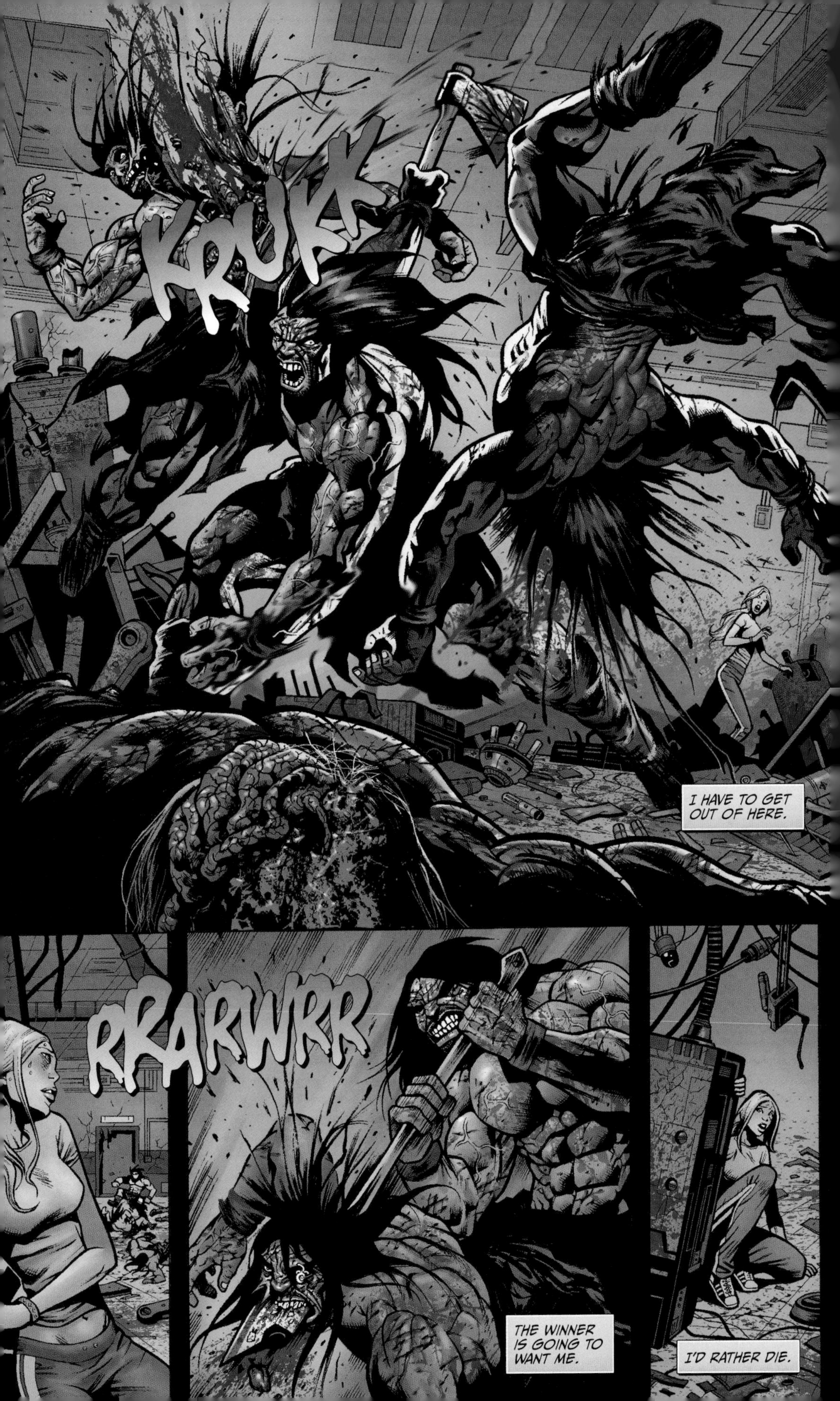
KRUKK
I HAVE TO GET OUT OF HERE.
RRARWRR
THE WINNER IS GOING TO WANT ME.
I'D RATHER DIE.

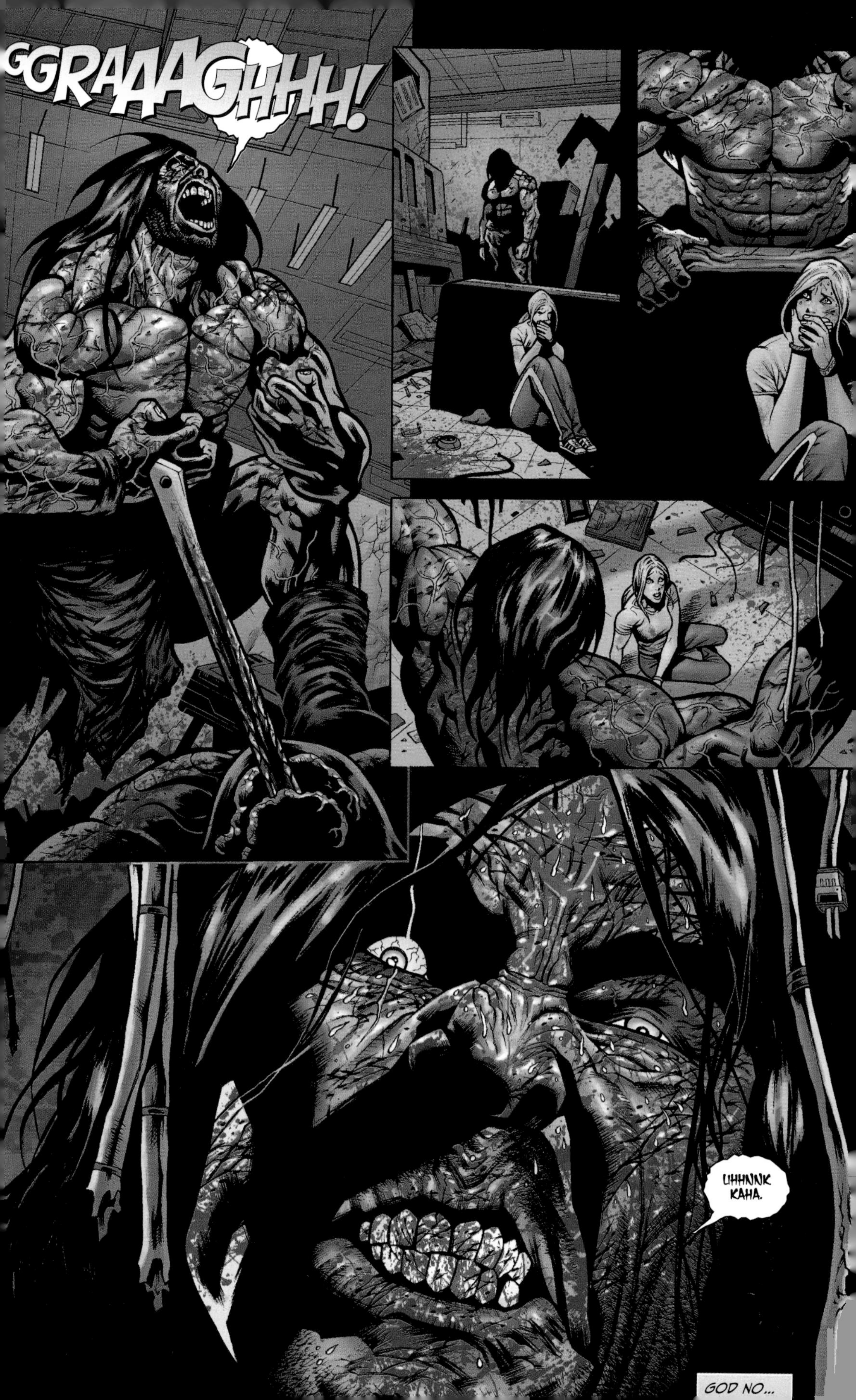
GGRAAAGHHH!
UHHNNK
KAHA.
GOD NO...

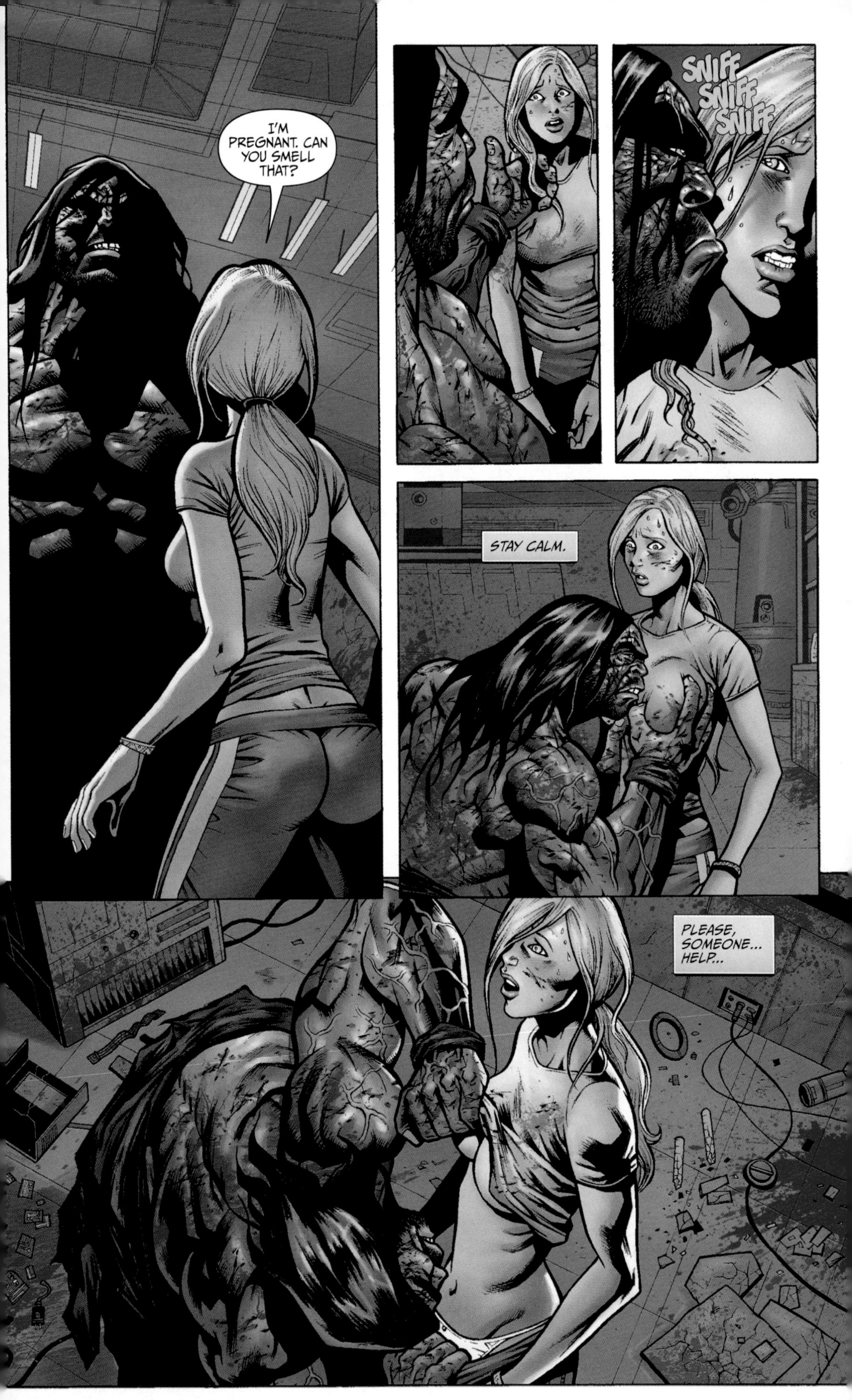

I'M PREGNANT. CAN YOU SMELL THAT?
SNIFF SNIFF SNIFF
STAY CALM.
PLEASE, SOMEONE... HELP...

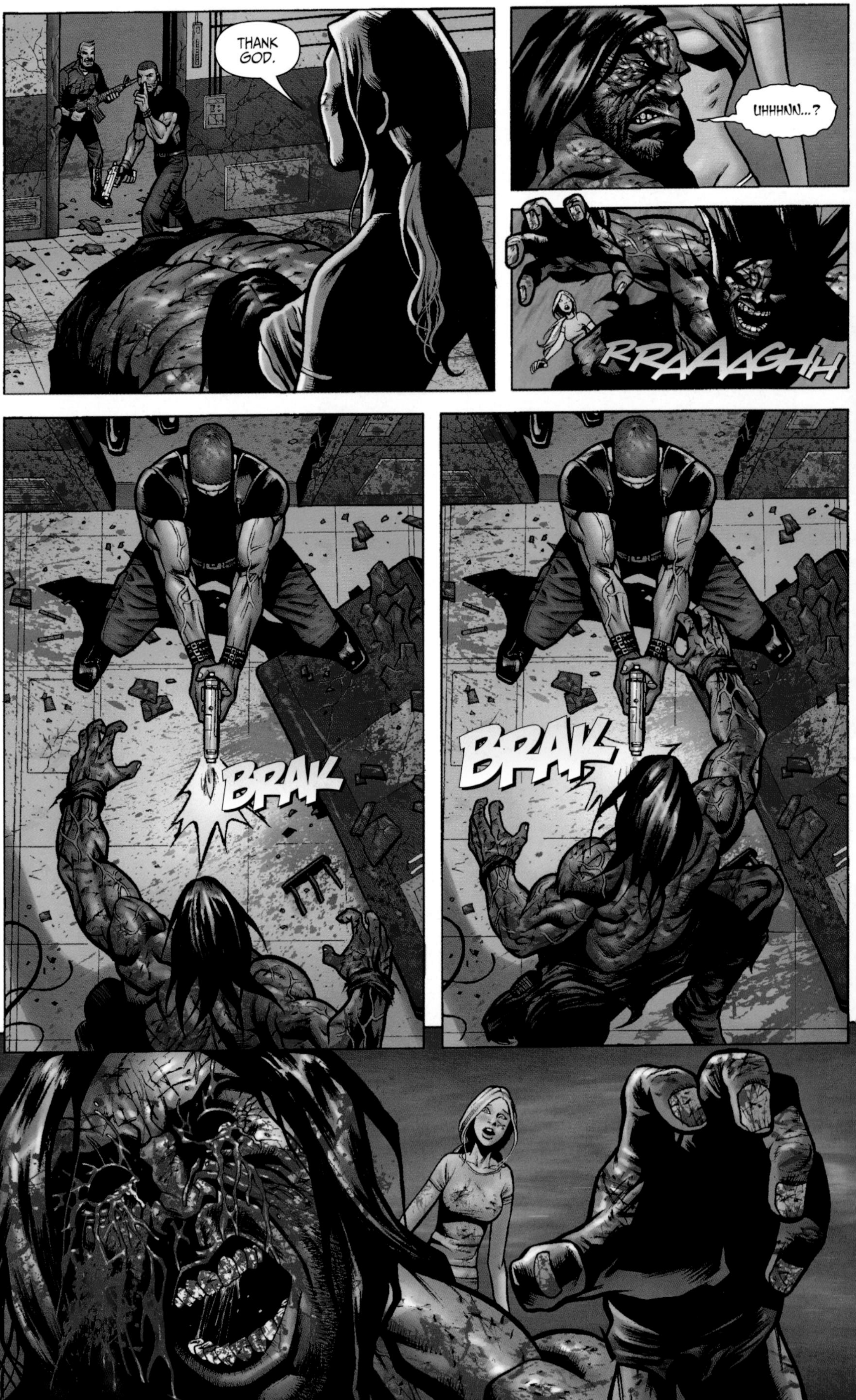

THANK GOD.
UHHHNN...?
RRAAAAGHH
BRAK
BRAK

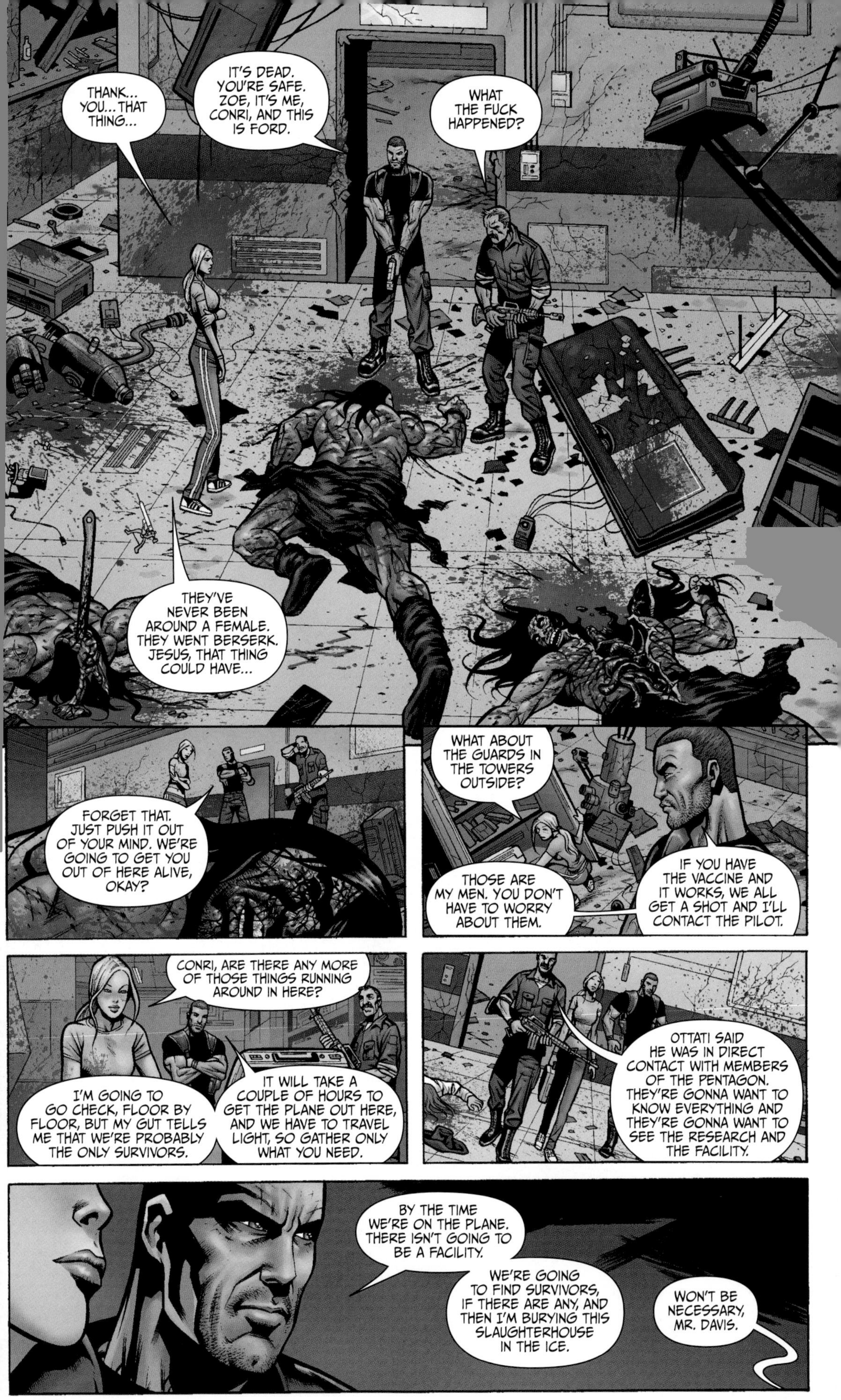
THANK... YOU...THAT THING...
IT'S DEAD. YOU'RE SAFE. ZOE, IT'S ME, CONRI, AND THIS IS FORD.
WHAT THE FUCK HAPPENED?
THEY'VE NEVER BEEN AROUND A FEMALE. THEY WENT BERSERK. JESUS, THAT THING COULD HAVE...
FORGET THAT. JUST PUSH IT OUT OF YOUR MIND. WE'RE GOING TO GET YOU OUT OF HERE ALIVE, OKAY?
WHAT ABOUT THE GUARDS IN THE TOWERS OUTSIDE?
THOSE ARE MY MEN. YOU DON'T HAVE TO WORRY ABOUT THEM.
IF YOU HAVE THE VACCINE AND IT WORKS, WE ALL GET A SHOT AND I'LL CONTACT THE PILOT.
CONRI, ARE THERE ANY MORE OF THOSE THINGS RUNNING AROUND IN HERE?
I'M GOING TO GO CHECK, FLOOR BY FLOOR, BUT MY GUT TELLS ME THAT WE'RE PROBABLY THE ONLY SURVIVORS.
IT WILL TAKE A COUPLE OF HOURS TO GET THE PLANE OUT HERE, AND WE HAVE TO TRAVEL LIGHT, SO GATHER ONLY WHAT YOU NEED.
OTTATI SAID HE WAS IN DIRECT CONTACT WITH MEMBERS OF THE PENTAGON. THEY'RE GONNA WANT TO KNOW EVERYTHING AND THEY'RE GONNA WANT TO SEE THE RESEARCH AND THE FACILITY.
BY THE TIME WE'RE ON THE PLANE. THERE ISN'T GOING TO BE A FACILITY.
WE'RE GOING TO FIND SURVIVORS, IF THERE ARE ANY, AND THEN I'M BURYING THIS SLAUGHTERHOUSE IN THE ICE.
WON'T BE NECESSARY, MR. DAVIS.

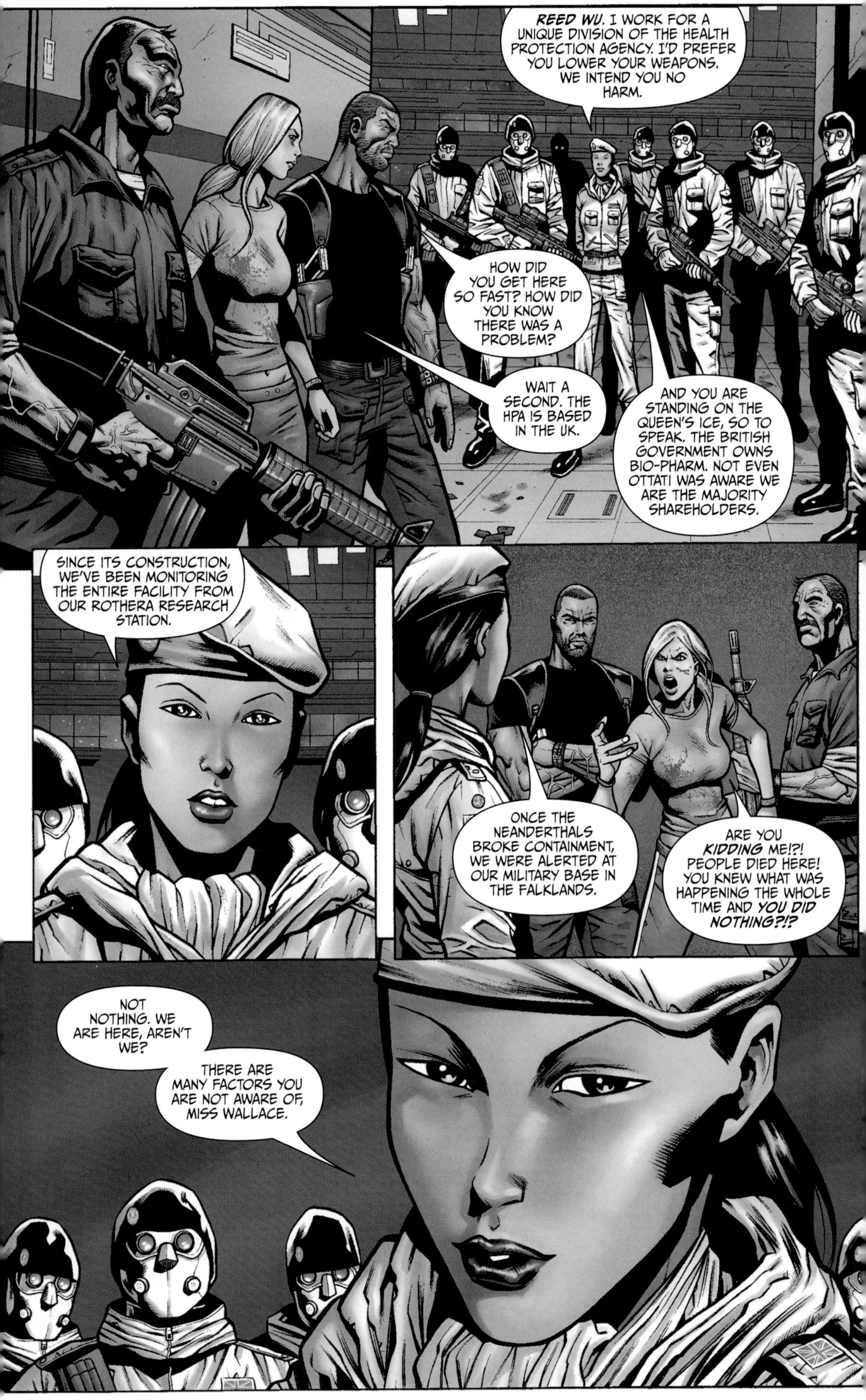
REED WU. I WORK FOR A UNIQUE DIVISION OF THE HEALTH PROTECTION AGENCY. I'D PREFER YOU LOWER YOUR WEAPONS. WE INTEND YOU NO HARM.
HOW DID YOU GET HERE SO FAST? HOW DID YOU KNOW THERE WAS A PROBLEM?
WAIT A SECOND. THE HPA IS BASED IN THE UK.
AND YOU ARE STANDING ON THE QUEEN'S ICE, SO TO SPEAK. THE BRITISH GOVERNMENT OWNS BIO-PHARM. NOT EVEN OTTATI WAS AWARE WE ARE THE MAJORITY SHAREHOLDERS.
SINCE ITS CONSTRUCTION, WE'VE BEEN MONITORING THE ENTIRE FACILITY FROM OUR ROTHERA RESEARCH STATION.
ONCE THE NEANDERTHALS BROKE CONTAINMENT, WE WERE ALERTED AT OUR MILITARY BASE IN THE FALKLANDS.
ARE YOU KIDDING ME!?! PEOPLE DIED HERE! YOU KNEW WHAT WAS HAPPENING THE WHOLE TIME AND YOU DID NOTHING?!?
NOT NOTHING. WE ARE HERE, AREN'T WE?
THERE ARE MANY FACTORS YOU ARE NOT AWARE OF, MISS WALLACE.

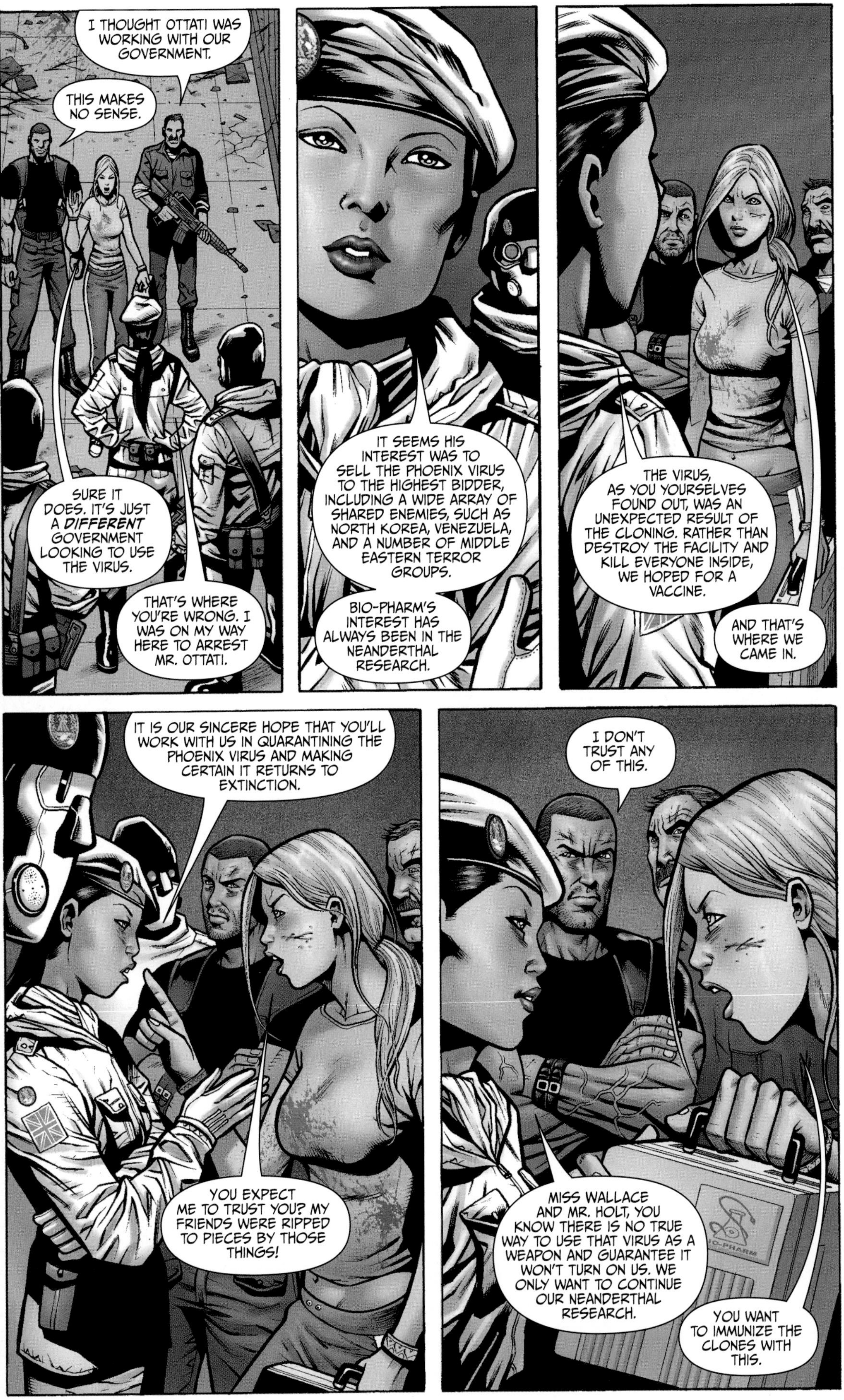
I THOUGHT OTTATI WAS WORKING WITH OUR GOVERNMENT.
THIS MAKES NO SENSE.
SURE IT DOES. IT'S JUST A *DIFFERENT* GOVERNMENT LOOKING TO USE THE VIRUS.
THAT'S WHERE YOU'RE WRONG. I WAS ON MY WAY HERE TO ARREST MR. OTTATI.
IT SEEMS HIS INTEREST WAS TO SELL THE PHOENIX VIRUS TO THE HIGHEST BIDDER, INCLUDING A WIDE ARRAY OF SHARED ENEMIES, SUCH AS NORTH KOREA, VENEZUELA, AND A NUMBER OF MIDDLE EASTERN TERROR GROUPS.
BIO-PHARM'S INTEREST HAS ALWAYS BEEN IN THE NEANDERTHAL RESEARCH.
THE VIRUS, AS YOU YOURSELVES FOUND OUT, WAS AN UNEXPECTED RESULT OF THE CLONING. RATHER THAN DESTROY THE FACILITY AND KILL EVERYONE INSIDE, WE HOPED FOR A VACCINE.
AND THAT'S WHERE WE CAME IN.
IT IS OUR SINCERE HOPE THAT YOU'LL WORK WITH US IN QUARANTINING THE PHOENIX VIRUS AND MAKING CERTAIN IT RETURNS TO EXTINCTION.
YOU EXPECT ME TO TRUST YOU? MY FRIENDS WERE RIPPED TO PIECES BY THOSE THINGS!
I DON'T TRUST ANY OF THIS.
MISS WALLACE AND MR. HOLT, YOU KNOW THERE IS NO TRUE WAY TO USE THAT VIRUS AS A WEAPON AND GUARANTEE IT WON'T TURN ON US. WE ONLY WANT TO CONTINUE OUR NEANDERTHAL RESEARCH.
YOU WANT TO IMMUNIZE THE CLONES WITH THIS.

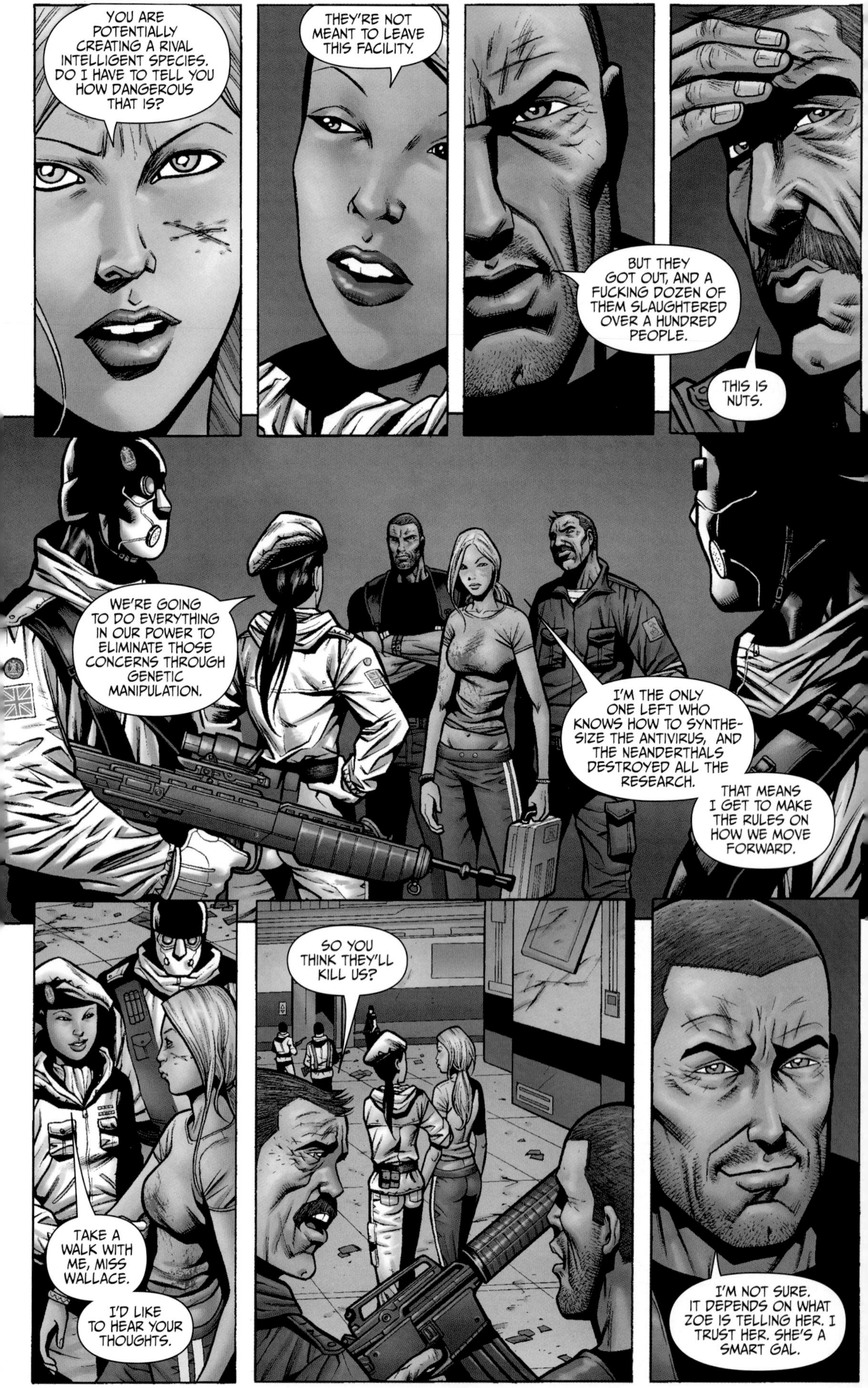
YOU ARE POTENTIALLY CREATING A RIVAL INTELLIGENT SPECIES. DO I HAVE TO TELL YOU HOW DANGEROUS THAT IS?
THEY'RE NOT MEANT TO LEAVE THIS FACILITY.
BUT THEY GOT OUT, AND A FUCKING DOZEN OF THEM SLAUGHTERED OVER A HUNDRED PEOPLE.
THIS IS NUTS.
WE'RE GOING TO DO EVERYTHING IN OUR POWER TO ELIMINATE THOSE CONCERNS THROUGH GENETIC MANIPULATION.
I'M THE ONLY ONE LEFT WHO KNOWS HOW TO SYNTHESIZE THE ANTIVIRUS, AND THE NEANDERTHALS DESTROYED ALL THE RESEARCH.
THAT MEANS I GET TO MAKE THE RULES ON HOW WE MOVE FORWARD.
TAKE A WALK WITH ME, MISS WALLACE.
I'D LIKE TO HEAR YOUR THOUGHTS.
SO YOU THINK THEY'LL KILL US?
I'M NOT SURE. IT DEPENDS ON WHAT ZOE IS TELLING HER. I TRUST HER. SHE'S A SMART GAL.

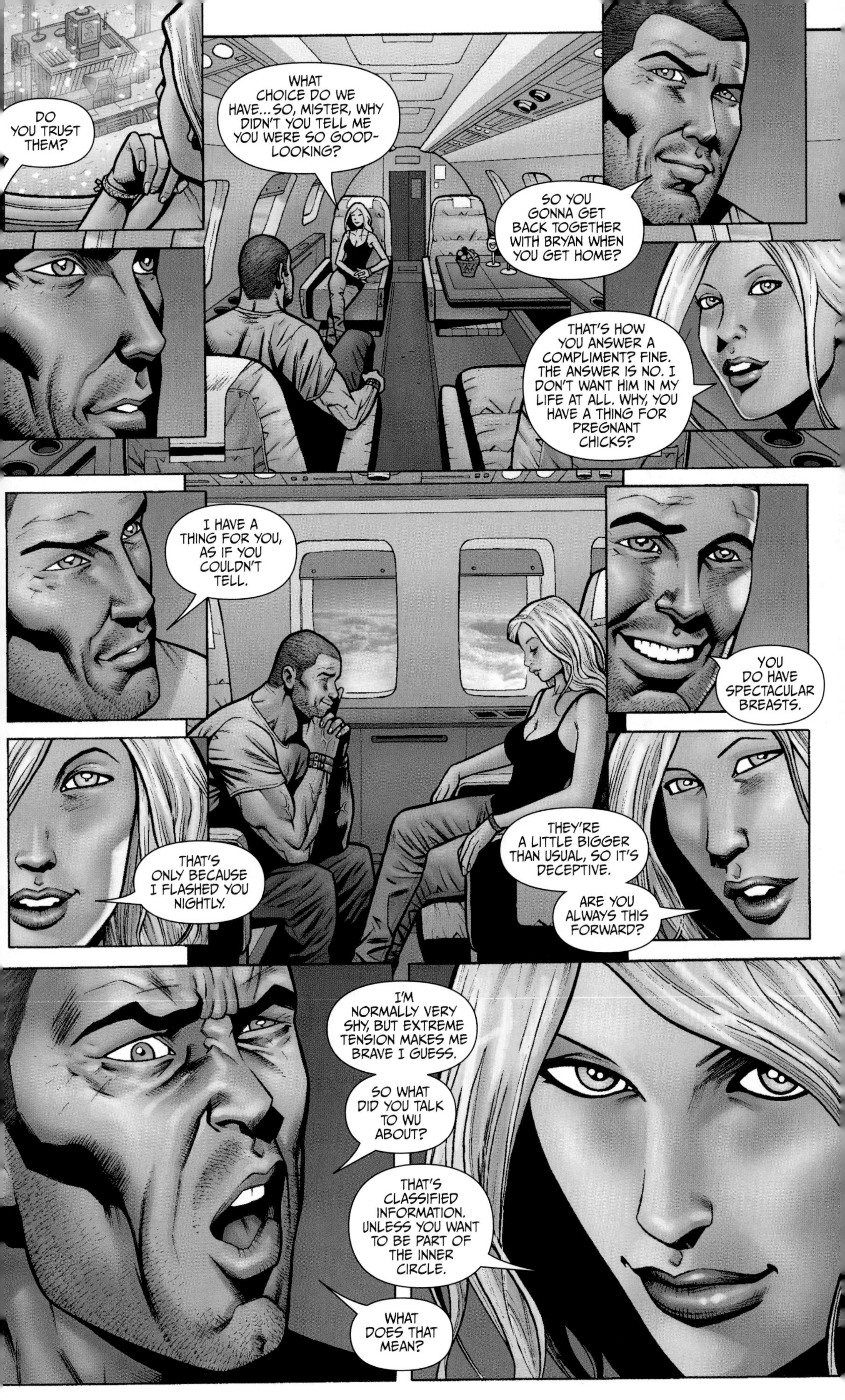

DO YOU TRUST THEM?
WHAT CHOICE DO WE HAVE...SO, MISTER, WHY DIDN'T YOU TELL ME YOU WERE SO GOOD-LOOKING?
SO YOU GONNA GET BACK TOGETHER WITH BRYAN WHEN YOU GET HOME?
THAT'S HOW YOU ANSWER A COMPLIMENT? FINE. THE ANSWER IS NO. I DON'T WANT HIM IN MY LIFE AT ALL. WHY, YOU HAVE A THING FOR PREGNANT CHICKS?
I HAVE A THING FOR YOU, AS IF YOU COULDN'T TELL.
YOU DO HAVE SPECTACULAR BREASTS.
THAT'S ONLY BECAUSE I FLASHED YOU NIGHTLY.
THEY'RE A LITTLE BIGGER THAN USUAL, SO IT'S DECEPTIVE.
ARE YOU ALWAYS THIS FORWARD?
I'M NORMALLY VERY SHY, BUT EXTREME TENSION MAKES ME BRAVE I GUESS.
SO WHAT DID YOU TALK TO WU ABOUT?
THAT'S CLASSIFIED INFORMATION. UNLESS YOU WANT TO BE PART OF THE INNER CIRCLE.
WHAT DOES THAT MEAN?

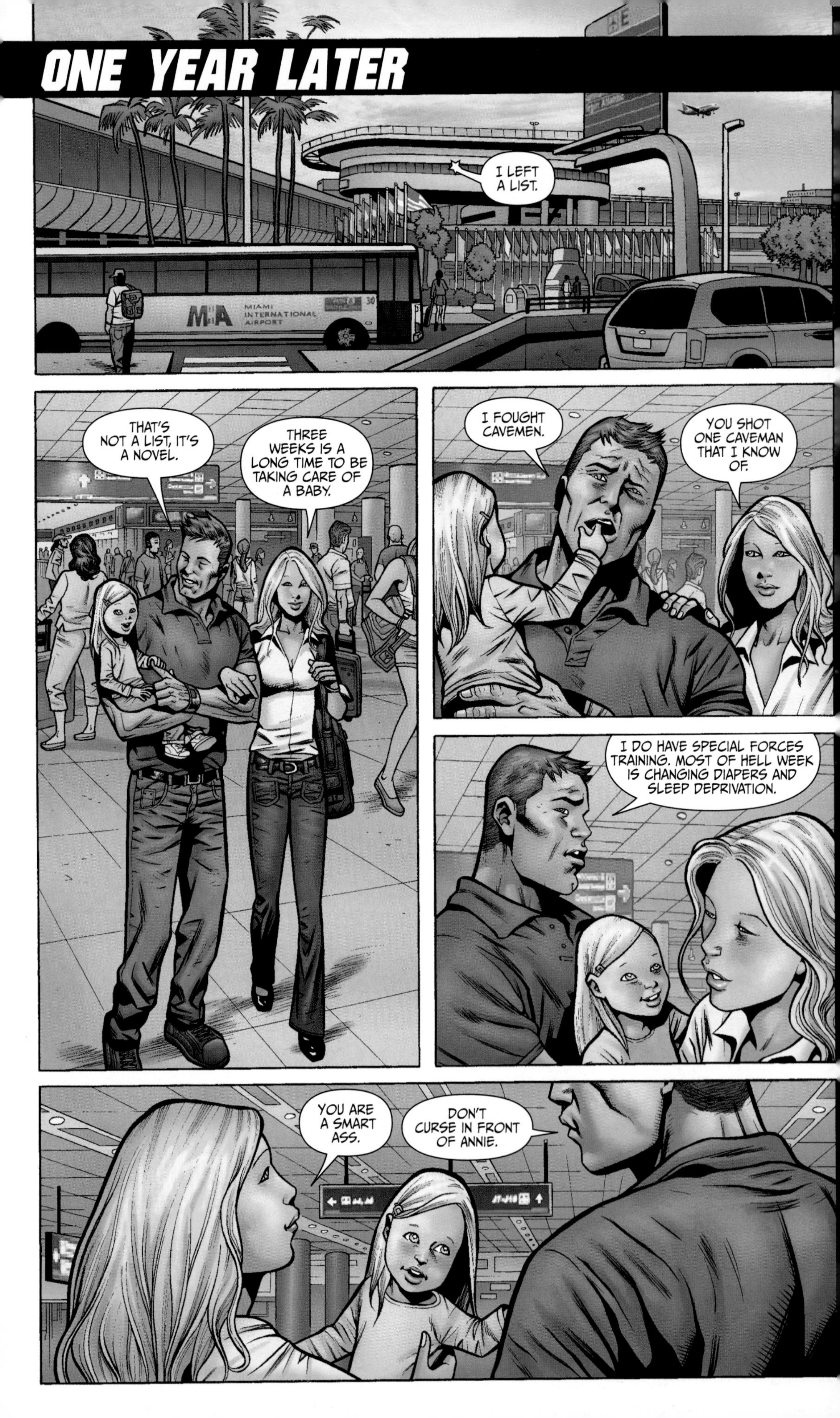
ONE YEAR LATER
MIAMI INTERNATIONAL AIRPORT
I LEFT A LIST.
THAT'S NOT A LIST, IT'S A NOVEL.
THREE WEEKS IS A LONG TIME TO BE TAKING CARE OF A BABY.
I FOUGHT CAVEMEN.
YOU SHOT ONE CAVEMAN THAT I KNOW OF.
I DO HAVE SPECIAL FORCES TRAINING. MOST OF HELL WEEK IS CHANGING DIAPERS AND SLEEP DEPRIVATION.
YOU ARE A SMART ASS.
DON'T CURSE IN FRONT OF ANNIE.

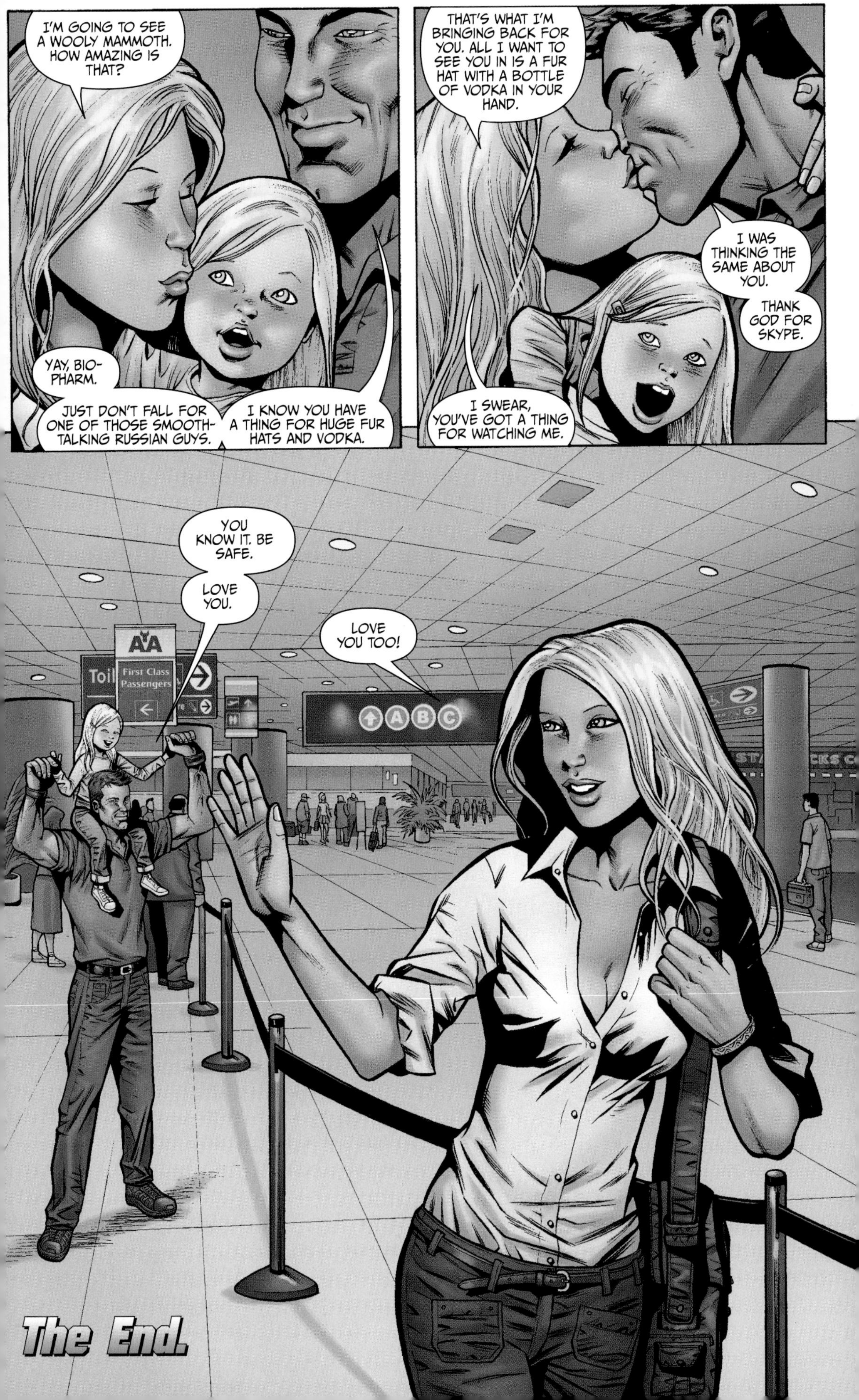
I'M GOING TO SEE A WOOLY MAMMOTH. HOW AMAZING IS THAT?
YAY, BIO-PHARM.
JUST DON'T FALL FOR ONE OF THOSE SMOOTH-TALKING RUSSIAN GUYS.
I KNOW YOU HAVE A THING FOR HUGE FUR HATS AND VODKA.
THAT'S WHAT I'M BRINGING BACK FOR YOU. ALL I WANT TO SEE YOU IN IS A FUR HAT WITH A BOTTLE OF VODKA IN YOUR HAND.
I WAS THINKING THE SAME ABOUT YOU.
THANK GOD FOR SKYPE.
I SWEAR, YOU'VE GOT A THING FOR WATCHING ME.
YOU KNOW IT. BE SAFE.
LOVE YOU.
LOVE YOU TOO!
AA
Toil
First Class Passengers
A B C
The End.

THANKS.

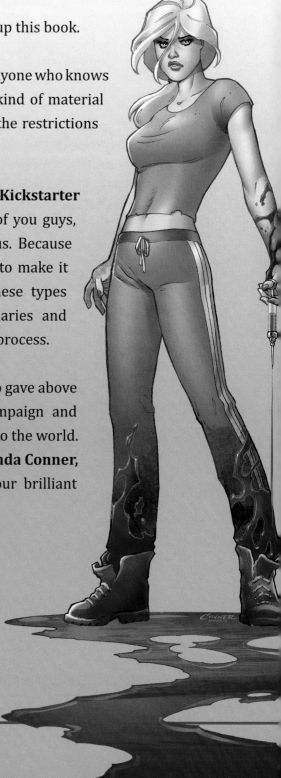

We wanted to thank you for picking up this book.

It's a bit of a departure for us, but to anyone who knows our work, it's probably exactly the kind of material you would expect from us, without the restrictions of a company behind us.

This book was entirely funded by a **Kickstarter** campaign, and is possible because of you guys, your generosity, and your faith in us. Because of this success, we are going to try to make it our business to do a couple of these types of projects a year, pushing boundaries and hopefully entertaining you all in the process.

To the right is a list of the people who gave above and beyond to the Kickstarter campaign and helped us get *Retrovirus* out there into the world. A special thank you goes out to **Amanda Conner, Paul Mounts**, **Bill Tortolini**, and our brilliant artist, **Norberto Fernandez**.

JIMMY PALMIOTTI
JUSTIN GRAY
OCTOBER 2012

THESE BACKERS HAD CHARACTERS NAMED FOR THEM:

Backer Name	Character Name
Scott M Davis	Conri Davis
Michael Amman	Bruno Jordan
Tate Ottati	Tate Ottati
Wendie Wu	Reed Wu

Scott Davis	Micah Baldwin
Ron Vink	Kimberly Urra
Damin Toell	Michael Amman
Don Brown	Tate Ottati
Henry & Wendie Wu	John Babshaw
Kristy Quinn	Nobuko Cobi Narita
Mikias Kekecs	Blake Domeyer
Stephanie Wooten	Jeffrey Tschiltsch
Calum Johnston	Daniel Paulson
Dana Rae	Susanne Fischer
Ben DeFeo	Martial Michel
Mathieu Doublet	John Balen
Gerald Mansfield	Andy Hampton
Peter McQuillan	Charles Joy
Marc Barrington	Michael Scuderi
Zoe Wadsworth	Anthony Tuason
David Ferguson	Joseph David
Russ Burlingame	Christopher Keszycki
David Mandel	Scott Wagner
Homer Frizzell	Georg Grosse-Hohl
James Santangelo	John Chambers
Mathias Hensler	Ranti Junus

Lastly, to the crew at **IMAGE COMICS** and everyone
else we may have missed: you *know* we love you.

NORBERTO'S
SKETCHBOOK

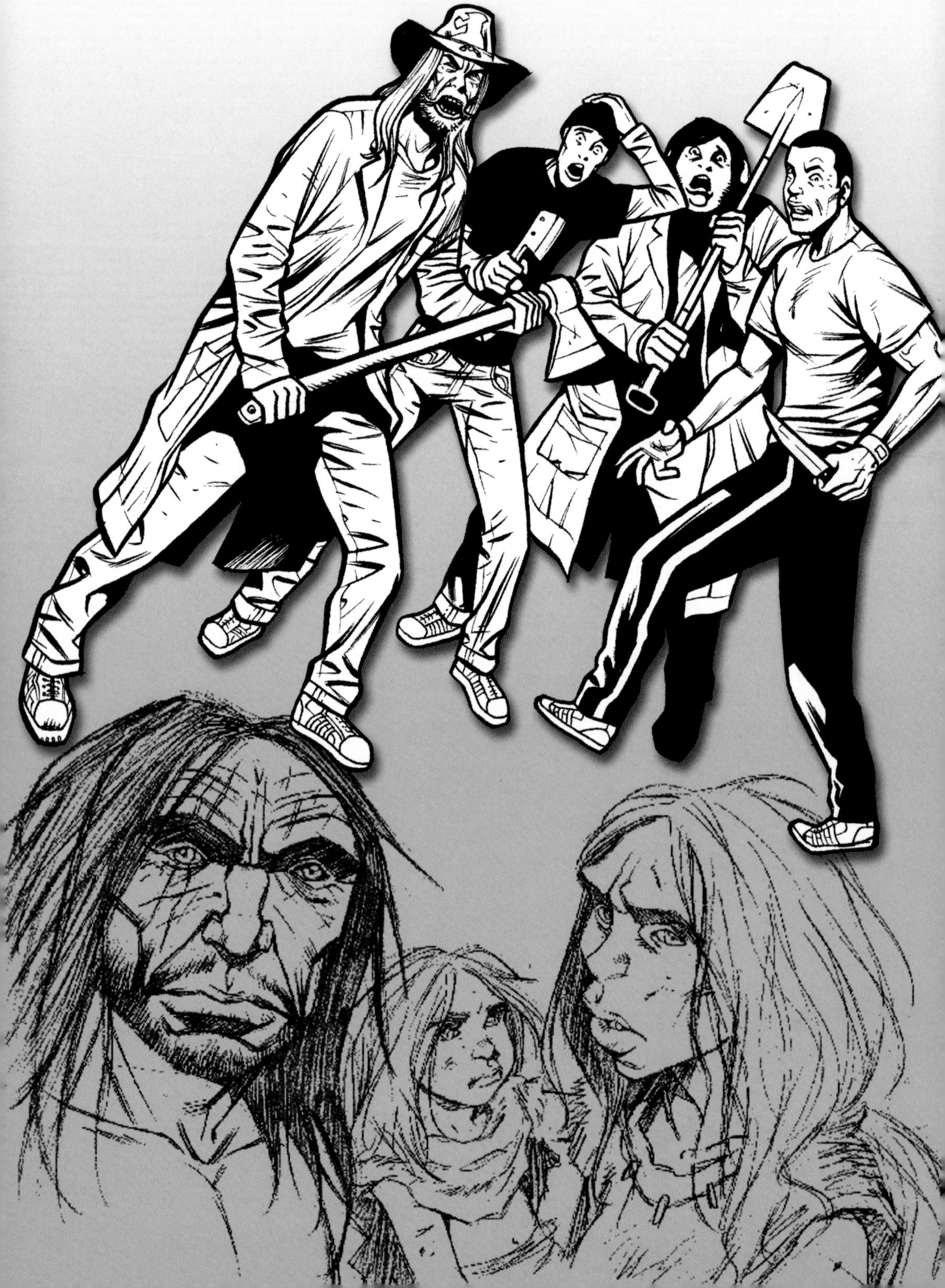

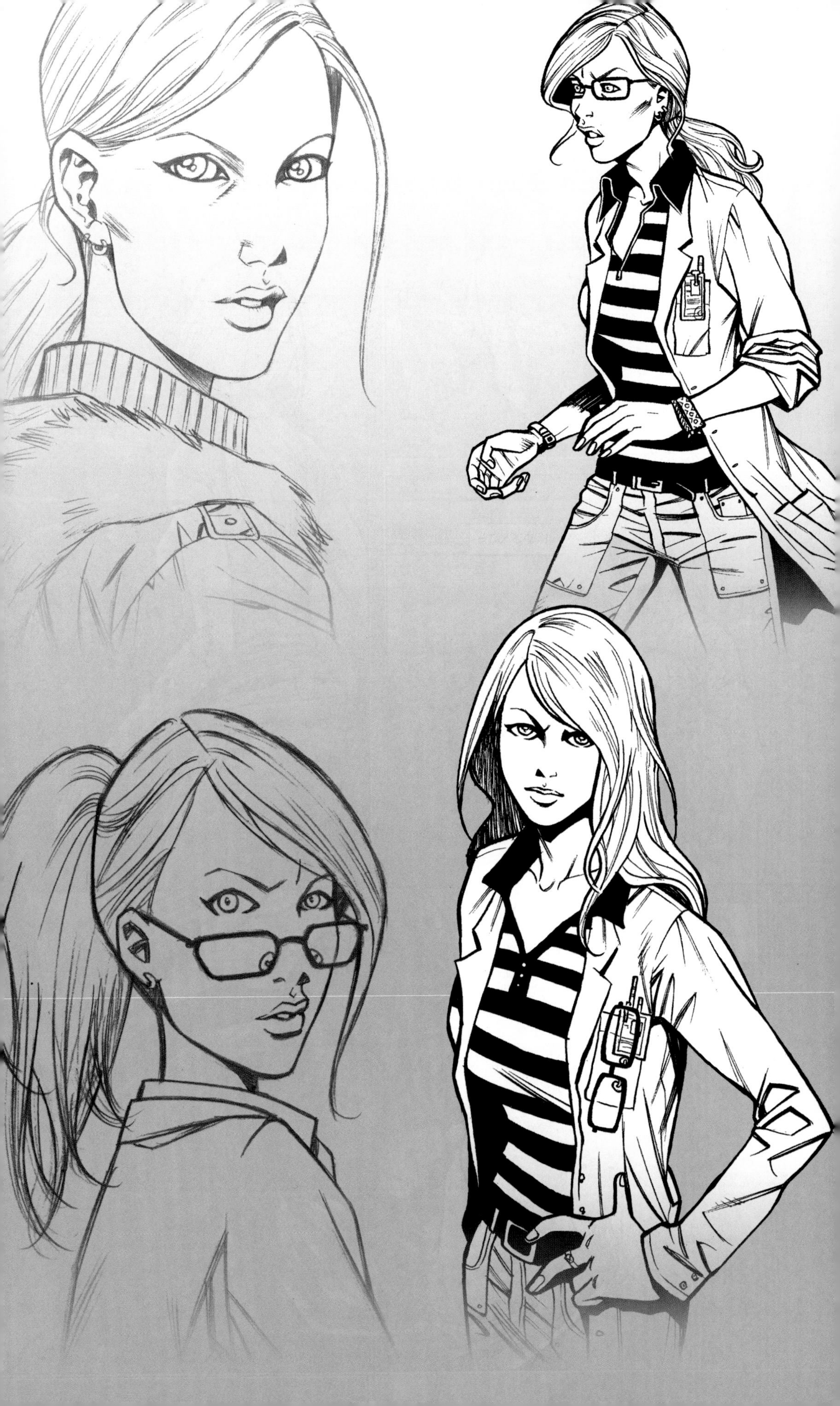

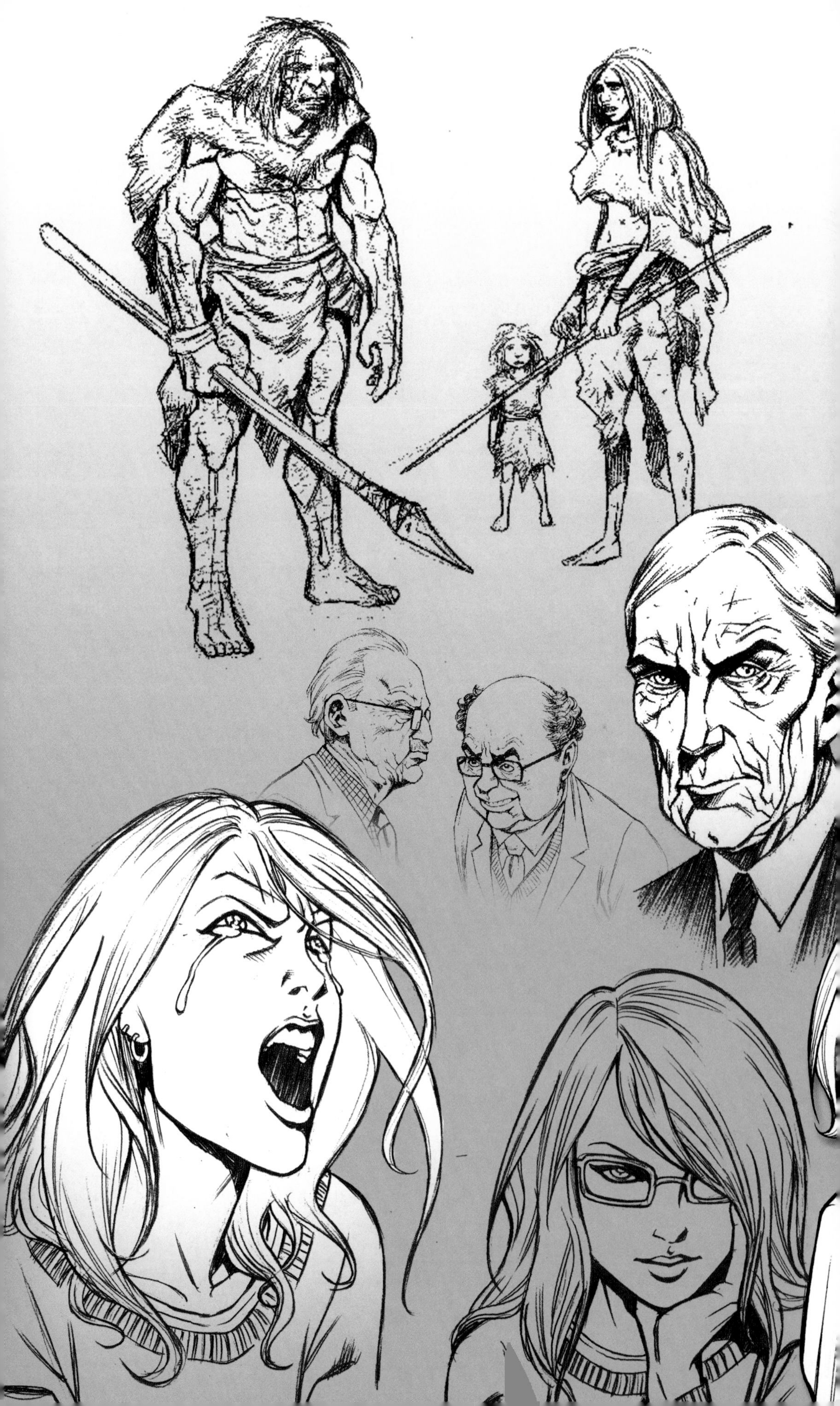

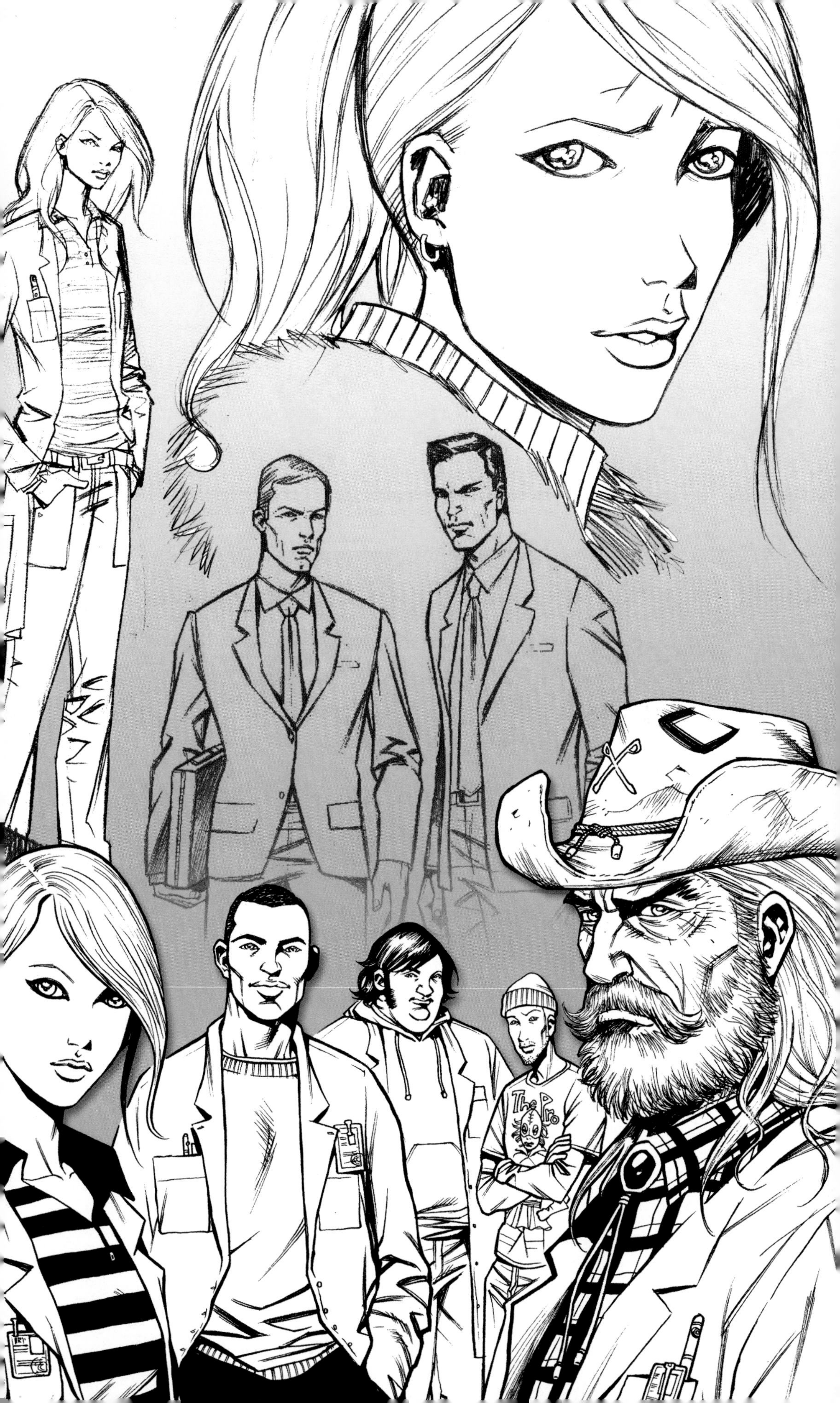
The Pro

JIMMY PALMIOTTI

Jimmy Palmiotti is a multi-award-winning character creator with a wide range of production, consulting, editorial, film-writing, development and production, media presentation, and video game development credits. Just a few of his clients include: **Nike, Nickelodeon, Universal Pictures, Disney, Warner Brothers, DreamWorks, Lionsgate, Vidmark, Starz, Fox Atomic, Alliance Films, New Line, Spike TV, MTV, 2k Games, Midway, Radical Games, Activision** and **THQ games.**

He is the co-founder of such companies as **Event Comics, Black Bull Media, Marvel Knights** (a division of Marvel Comics), and the current **Paperfilms**, where he is partners with Amanda Conner and Justin Gray. Together they have created and co-created numerous universes, comics, TV series and characters including: *The New West, Monolith, 21 Down, The Resistance, The Pro, Gatecrasher, Beautiful Killer, Ash, Cloudburst, Trigger Girl 6, Thrill Seeker, Trailblazer, Ballerina, The Twilight Experiment,* and the TV series *Painkiller Jane.*

Current work includes: *All-Star Western* for **DC Comics;** *The Last Resort* for **IDW;** *The Tattered Man, TrailBlazer, Back to Brooklyn* and *Random Acts of Violence* for **Image Comics;** and *Time Bomb* for **Radical Comics.**

JUSTIN GRAY

Over the last decade, Justin Gray has worked on comicbook titles that include *Power Girl, 21Down, Jonah Hex, Marvel Adventures, The Monolith, Daughters of the Dragon,* and *Tattered Man.*

He's also written for children's magazines, film, television, and video games.

Prior to his work as a professional author, Justin was a fossil hunter, advocate for victims of crime, and a microphotographer capturing rare images of 20-million-year-old insects trapped in amber.

NORBERTO FERNANDEZ

Born in Vigo (Spain) in 1967, after some years working in a bank, Norberto made the decision to work full-time on comic books and illustration. He started working in local newspapers on strips named *Guinsy* and *Forest Hill,* written by Carlos Portela.

Later, he published *Fabulas Benevolas* (at **Kaleidoscope**) and worked for adult magazines like *Penthouse Comix* and *Eros Comix,* as well as at *El Vibora Magazine,* with the series *Broz.*

Norberto also worked on the kids magazine *Golfiño,* with the series *El Castillo Regadera* (edited by el Patito Editorial), *Las Aventuras de Xiana* and *Percy y Marionetti* (writen by David Gundin).

With Ediciones Dolmen, Norberto published the monographic called *Quatroccento,* while also working as an illustrator for books and for publicity.

Norberto has also worked at **Marvel** as an inker, and at **Zenescope** doing covers.

BILL TORTOLINI

Already an accomplished art director and graphic designer, Bill began designing and lettering in the comic industry more than a decade ago and has worked with many of comics' top creators and publishers including **Marvel, IDW, Image, Kickstart, MTV,** and **Del Rey.**

Current and past projects include: *Stephen King's Talisman, Anita Blake: Vampire Hunter, Army of Darkness, Random Acts of Violence, Back to Brooklyn, The Hedge Knight, Magician: Riftwar, Battlestar Galactica, The Wheel of Time, The Dresden Files, Transformers, Star Trek, G.I. Joe, The Last Resort, Archie Comics, True Blood, Trailblazer, Shock Rockets, Tattered Man* and many others.

Bill is an avid sports fan and lives in Massachusetts with his wife and three children.